THE RENAISSANCE

Studies in European History

General Editor: Richard Overy
Editorial Consultants: John Breuilly
Roy Porter

THE RENAISSANCE

PETER BURKE

Fellow of Emmanuel College, Cambridge

HUMANITIES PRESS INTERNATIONAL, INC.
Atlantic Highlands, NJ

First published in 1987 in the United States of America by
HUMANITIES PRESS INTERNATIONAL, INC.,
Atlantic Highlands, NJ 07716

Reprinted 1989, 1990

Library of Congress Cataloging-in-Publication Data
Burke, Peter
    The Renaissance.
    (Studies in European history)
    Bibliography: p.
    Includes Index.
    1. Renaissance.   I. Title.   II. Series: Studies in
European History (Atlantic Highlands, N.J.)
CB361.B8   1987   940.2'1   86-18571
ISBN 0-391-03484-7

PRINTED IN HONG KONG

Contents

List of Plates

1. Self portrait of Martin van Heemskerck: courtesy of the Fitzwilliam Museum, Cambridge.
2. Bramante's Tempietto: courtesy of the Mansell Collection.
3. Botticelli's *Calumny*: courtesy of the Mansell Collection.
4. Michelangelo's Bacchus: courtesy of the Mansell Collection.
5. The Patheon in Rome: courtesy of the Mansell Collection.
6. Diagram from Bovillus, *De Sapiente*: courtesy of the British Library.

Editor's Preface

The main purpose of this new series of studies is to make available to teacher and student alike developments in a field of history that has become increasingly specialized with the sheer volume of new research and literature now produced. These studies are designed to present the "state of the debate" on important themes and episodes in European history since the sixteenth century, presented in a clear and critical way by someone who is closely concerned himself with the debate in question.

The studies are not intended to be read as extended bibliographical essays, though each will contain a detailed guide to further reading which will lead students and the general reader quickly to key publications. Each book carries its own interpretation and conclusions, while locating the discussion firmly in the center of the current issues as historians see them. It is intended that the series will introduce students to historical approaches which are in some cases very new and which, in the normal course of things, would take many years to filter down into the textbooks and school histories. I hope it will demonstrate some of the excitement historians, like scientists, feel as they work away in the vanguard of their subject.

The format of the series conforms closely with that of the companion volumes of studies in economic and social history which has already established a major reputation since its inception in 1968. Both series have an important contribution to make in publicizing what it is that historians are doing and in making history more open and accessible. It is vital for history to communicate if it is to survive.

R.J. OVERY

1   The Myth of the Renaissance

'At the sound of the word "Renaissance"', wrote the Dutch historian Johan Huizinga, 'the dreamer of past beauty sees purple and gold' [9]. More exactly, he or she sees in the mind's eye Botticelli's *Birth of Venus*, Michelangelo's *David*, Leonardo's *Mona Lisa*, Erasmus, the châteaux of the Loire, and the *Faerie Queene*, all rolled into one, into a composite picture of a golden age of creativity and culture.

This image of the Renaissance – with a capital R – goes back to the middle of the nineteenth century, to the French historian Jules Michelet (who loved it), to the critic John Ruskin (who disapproved) and, above all, to the Swiss scholar Jacob Burckhardt, whose famous *Civilisation of the Renaissance in Italy* (1860), defined the period in terms of two concepts, 'individualism' and 'modernity'. 'In the Middle Ages', according to Burckhardt, 'human consciousness ... lay dreaming or half awake beneath a common veil ... Man was conscious of himself only as a member of a race, people, party, family, or corporation – only through some general category.' In Renaissance Italy, however, 'this veil first melted into air ... man became a spiritual *individual*, and recognised himself as such' [1: part 2]. Renaissance meant modernity. The Italian was, Burckhardt wrote, 'the first-born among the sons of modern Europe'. The fourteenth-century poet Petrarch was 'one of the first truly modern men'. The great renewal of art and ideas began in Italy, and at a later stage the new attitudes and the new artistic forms spread to the rest of Europe.

This idea of the Renaissance is a myth. 'Myth' is, of course, an ambiguous term and it is deliberately used here in two different senses. When professional historians refer to 'myths', they usually mean statements about the past which they can show to be false, or at any rate misleading. In the case of

1

Burckhardt's account of the Renaissance, they object to the dramatic contrasts which he makes between Renaissance and Middle Ages and between Italy and the rest of Europe. They consider these contrasts to be exaggerated, ignoring as they do the many innovations which were made in the Middle Ages; the survival of traditional attitudes into the sixteenth century, or even later; and Italian interest in the painting and music of the Netherlands.

The second sense of the term 'myth' is a more literary one. A myth is a symbolic story told about characters who are larger (or blacker, or whiter) than life; a story with a moral, and in particular a story about the past which is told in order to explain or justify some present state of affairs. Burckhardt's Renaissance is a myth in this sense too. The characters in his story, whether they are heroes like Alberti and Michelangelo or villains like the Borgias, are all larger than life. The story itself both explains and justifies the modern world. It is a symbolic story in the sense that it describes cultural change in terms of the metaphors of awakening and rebirth. These metaphors are not merely decorative. They are essential to Burckhardt's interpretation.

These metaphors were not new in Burckhardt's day. From the middle of the fourteenth century onwards, a growing number of scholars, writers and artists in Italy and elsewhere came to use the imagery of renewal to mark their sense of living in a new age, an age of regeneration, renovation, restoration, recall, rebirth, reawakening, or re-emergence into light after what they were the first to call the 'dark ages'.

The metaphors were not new in their day either. The Roman poet Virgil paints a vivid picture of the return of the golden age in his Fourth Eclogue, while the idea of rebirth is clearly expressed in the Gospel of St John: 'Unless a man be born again of water and the Holy Ghost, he cannot enter into the kingdom of God.' If anything was distinctive about the use of these metaphors in the period 1300–1600, with which we are mainly concerned, it was their application to a scholarly or artistic movement, rather than to a political or religious one. In the 1430s, for example, Leonardo Bruni described Petrarch as the first 'who possessed such grace and genius that he could recognise and recall to the light the

2

ancient elegance of style, which had been lost and extinguished'. Erasmus told pope Leo X that 'our age ... bids fair to be an age of gold' thanks to the revival of learning as well as piety, while Giorgio Vasari organised his *Lives* of painters, sculptors and architects around the idea of a renewal of the arts in three stages from the beginnings in the age of Giotto to the culminating points of Leonardo, Raphael and, above all, Vasari's own master Michelangelo.

Like all self-images, that of the scholars and artists of the Renaissance was both revealing and misleading. Like other sons rebelling against their fathers' generation, these men owed a great deal to the 'Middle Ages' they so frequently denounced. If they overestimated their distance from the recent past, they underestimated their distance from the remote past, the antiquity they admired so much. Their account of their rebirth was a myth in the sense that it presented a misleading account of the past; that it was a dream, a wish-fulfilment; and that it was a re-enactment or representation of the ancient myth of the eternal return [10: ch.x].

Burckhardt's mistake was to accept the scholars and artists of the period at their own valuation, to take this story of rebirth at its face value and to elaborate it into a book. To the old formulae of the restoration of the arts and the revival of classical antiquity, he added new ones such as individualism, realism, and modernity. E.H. Carr's adage, 'Before you study history, study the historian' is good advice in Burckhardt's case. There were doubtless personal reasons for his attraction to the period and to this image of it. Burckhardt saw Italy, past and present, as an escape from a Switzerland he found dull and stuffy. In his youth he sometimes signed his name in Italian as 'Giacomo Burcardo'. He described himself as a good private individual', as well as characterising the Renaissance as an age of individualism. These personal reasons do not of course explain the success of the new definition, or the growing interest in the Renaissance in the later nineteenth century (among intellectuals such as Walter Pater, Robert Browning and John Addington Symonds in England and their equivalents abroad). To account for this success we need to evoke the quasi-religious cult of the arts in newly-built temples called 'museums', and also the concern with 'realism' and 'individualism' on the part of nineteenth-century artists and writers. Like Erasmus and Vasari, they projected their ideals on to the past, creating their own myth of a golden age, a cultural miracle.

This nineteenth-century myth of the Renaissance is still taken seriously by many people. Television companies and organisers of package tours still make money out of it. However, professional historians have become dissatisfied with this version of the Renaissance, even if they continue to find the period and the movement attractive. The point is that the grand edifice erected by Burckhardt and his contemporaries has not stood the test of time. More exactly, it has been undermined by the researches of the medievalists in particular [10: ch. xi]. Their arguments depend on innumerable points of detail, but they are of two main kinds.

In the first place, there are arguments to the effect that so-called 'Renaissance men' were really rather medieval. They were more traditional in their behaviour, assumptions and ideals than we tend to think – and also more traditional than they saw themselves. Hindsight suggests that even Petrarch, 'one of the first truly modern men', according to Burckhardt, and a figure who will recur in these pages because of his creativity as a poet and a scholar alike, had many attitudes in common with the centuries he described as 'dark' [72]. Two of the most famous books written in sixteenth-century Italy, the *Courtier* and the *Prince*, have turned out to be closer to the Middle Ages than they appear. Castiglione's *Courtier* draws on medieval traditions of courtly behaviour and courtly love as well as on classical texts like Plato's *Symposium* and Cicero *On Duties* [63]. Even Machiavelli's *Prince*, which deliberately turns the conventional wisdom on its head on occasion, belongs in a sense to a medieval genre, that of the so-called 'mirrors' or books of advice to rulers [29, 68].

In the second place, the medievalists have accumulated arguments to the effect that the Renaissance was not such a singular event as Burckhardt and his contemporaries once thought and that the term should really be used in the plural. There were various 'renascences' in the Middle Ages, notably in the twelfth century and in the age of Charlemagne. In both cases there was a combination of literary and artistic achievements with a revival of interest in classical learning, and in both cases contemporaries described their age as one of restoration, rebirth or 'renovation' [4, 78].

Some bold spirits, notably the late Arnold Toynbee in his *Study of History*, have gone further still in this direction and discovered renascences outside western Europe, whether in Byzantium, the world of Islam, or even in the Far East. 'In using the word renaissance as a proper name', wrote Toynbee, 'we have been allowing ourselves to fall into the error of seeing a unique occurrence in an event which in reality was no more than one particular instance of a recurrent historical phenomenon' [88]. His 'no more than' reduces a complex movement to one of its traits, but Toynbee is surely right to try to place the Renaissance in world history, and to draw attention to the revivals of 'Hellenism' (as he calls the classical tradition) outside western Europe, and also to revivals of 'dead' indigenous traditions in China and Japan. Each revival had its specific features, just like an individual person; but all the revivals are in a sense members of the same 'family'.

Where does this leave us? Was there a Renaissance at all? If we describe the 'Renaissance' in purple and gold, as an isolated cultural miracle, or as the sudden emergence of modernity, my own answer would be 'no'. If, however, the term is used, without prejudice to the achievements of the Middle Ages, or those of the world beyond Europe, to refer to a particular cluster of changes in western culture, then it may be regarded as an organising concept which still has its uses. To describe and interpret this cluster of changes is the task of the remainder of this essay.

2 Italy: Revival and Innovation

Despite the need to revise the accepted account of the Renaissance, which presents Italy as active and creative and the rest of Europe as passive and imitative, it is impossible not to start with Italy. This section is therefore concerned with the principal changes in the arts, literature and ideas from Giotto (d.1337) to Tintoretto (1518–94), and from Petrarch (1304–74) to Tasso (1544–95). It will attempt to place these changes – whether revivals or innovations – in their cultural and social context. It is obvious enough that there was no lack of creative individuals in this period, men (they were indeed males for the most part) who impressed their personalities on their works. All the same, if we look at the course of cultural change in Italy over the long term, over the three hundred years 1300–1600, it becomes equally obvious that the achievements are collective in the sense that small groups worked together and each generation built on the work of its predecessors. In a relatively brief essay it seems best to stress the collective and to try to see the Renaissance movement as a whole.

What is especially distinctive about this movement is the whole-hearted attempt to revive another culture, to imitate antiquity in many different fields and media. This is not the only important feature of the Italian Renaissance, but it may not be a bad place to begin.

The revival of classical forms is most obvious in architecture, from the ground-plans to the ornamental details [83: chs 26–7). It is no surprise that this revival of Greek and Roman architecture should have taken place in Italy, where a number of classical buildings had survived more or less intact, including the Pantheon (Plate 5), the Colosseum, the Arch of Constantine and the Theatre of Marcellus (all in Rome itself)

7

while the climate made the imitation of these buildings more practical in the south of Europe than it could be elsewhere. Generations of architects, including Filippo Brunelleschi (1377-1446), Donato Bramante (c.1444—1514), and Andrea Palladio (1508—80), went to Rome to study and measure these buildings in order to imitate the principles on which they were built. Their studies were assisted by the survival of a treatise on architecture written by an ancient Roman, Vitruvius. His *Ten Books of Architecture* was first published in 1486 or thereabouts. Vitruvius emphasised the need for symmetry and proportion in architecture, comparing the structure of a building to that of the human body. He also explained the rules for the correct employment of the 'three orders', in other words the Doric, Ionic and Corinthian columns with their appropriate friezes, cornices and so on. The classical system of proportions was followed in such buildings as Brunelleschi's churches of San Lorenzo and Santo Spirito in Florence, and Leon Battista Alberti's San Francesco at Rimini. Bramante's San Pietro in Montorio in Rome, built in 1502 (Plate 2), broke with the traditional medieval cruciform church plan to follow the circular plan of a typical Roman temple; hence its Italian nickname of the 'little temple' (*Tempietto*). It was also the first church to utilise the full Doric order. Also reminiscent of a Roman temple is the grand portico of Palladio's Villa Foscari, nicknamed *La Malcontenta*, built at Fusina, not far from Venice, a little before 1560. In this case the order utilised is the Ionic. Roman country houses or villas had not survived, so Renaissance villas, from Poggio a Caiano in the 1480s to Pratolino in the 1570s (both built for the Medici family), drew on the descriptions of his country houses and gardens in the letters of the ancient Roman writer Pliny the younger [21, 22, 23].

In the case of sculpture, there was no ancient treatise like that of Vitruvius, but classical models were of enormous importance all the same [18, 19]. The sculptor Donatello went to Rome, like his friend Brunelleschi, in order to study the remains of classical antiquity, while Buonaccolsi (nick-named *Antico*), who became famous for his small bronzes, was sent to Rome by his patron, the marquis of Mantua, for the same reason. By 1500 it had become fashionable for Italians of taste to collect classical marbles, and one of the greatest enthusiasts was pope Julius II. Julius owned most of the masterpieces which had been unearthed in his time, including the Belvedere Apollo (named after the papal villa in which it was displayed), and the still more famous Laocoön, which illustrates a scene from Homer's *Iliad*, in which a Trojan priest is crushed by serpents sent by Apollo. The new genres of Renaissance sculpture were generally classical genres revived, such as the portrait bust, the equestrian monument, and the figure or group illustrating classical mythology, such as the young Michelangelo's Bacchus (Plate 4), which imitated the classical style with such success that it was believed for a time to be a genuine antique.

In the case of painting, ancient sources and models were much harder to find. There was no equivalent of Vitruvius or even the Laocoön. Apart from a few decorations in Nero's Golden House at Rome, classical painting was unknown at this time, and would remain so until the excavation of Pompeii in the late eighteenth century. Like their colleagues in architecture and sculpture, painters wished (or were encouraged by their patrons) to imitate the ancients, but they had to use more indirect means, posing figures in the positions of famous classical sculptures, or attempting to reconstruct lost classical paintings from descriptions in literary texts [3, 12]. Botticelli's *Calumny*, for example (Plate 3), follows the description of a lost work by the painter Apelles given by the Greek writer Lucian. There was also an attempt to derive rules for painters from the literary criticism of the ancients, on the principle that, as Horace put it, 'as is painting, so is poetry'. Music was another art in which attempts were made — especially in the 1540s and 1550s — to recreate the ancient style on the basis of literary sources, in this case classical treatises [53].

The rise of the portrait as an independent genre was one of the trends which was encouraged by the example of antiquity. Fifteenth-century portraits were usually painted in profile as if imitating the heads of emperors on Roman coins, and they were usually cut short below the shoulders as if they were equivalents of classical marble busts. It was only around the year 1500 that Leonardo, Raphael and other artists emancipated themselves from this convention, to produce works without classical precedent which showed the sitter in full- or three-quarter-face, half- or full-length, sitting or standing, conversing with friends or giving orders to servants [75].

In painting, however, there was at least one crucial development of the period which took place without reference to antiquity; the discovery of the rules of linear perspective. It is possible that classical artists had known these rules, but they were lost until their rediscovery, by Brunelleschi and his friends, in the fifteenth century, an example which illustrates the affinity between the two ages and suggests that the similarities between them cannot be explained in terms of imitation alone [18].

In both classical and Renaissance times, artists were particularly concerned with the appearance of things, with what Burckhardt called 'realism'. The word is left in inverted commas not only because it has more than one meaning (illusionistic style; subject-matter taken from 'real life', whatever that is; and so on), but also because all artists represent what is real to them and because there can be no art without conventions. Even perspective can be regarded, in the words of the art historian Erwin Panofsky, as a 'symbolic form'. In other words, representing the world according to its rules meant accepting certain values and rejecting others [18].

In the case of medieval artists, these values have to be inferred from their work, with the consequent danger of a circular argument. Even in the case of Giotto, his concern with three-dimensionality, more especially the solidity of the human figure, has to be inferred in this way. In Italy in the fifteenth and sixteenth centuries, however, artists and others not infrequently expressed their ideas about art in writing and even, at the end of the period, in print, in Vasari's *Lives* and elsewhere. They make very clear what problems they were attempting to solve in their art and also their appreciation of such qualities as 'truth' to nature, the illusion of life, the apparently effortless overcoming of difficulties, and, hardest of all to define, 'grace' [6: ch. 6; 15].

Architecture, painting and sculpture have been discussed first because it is of the visual arts that most of us now think first when we hear the word 'Renaissance'. In the period itself, however, literature and learning, the so-called 'liberal arts' were taken more seriously (at least by the learned), than the 'mechanical arts', a category in which painting, sculpture and architecture were lumped together with agriculture, weaving and navigation, despite the protests of Leonardo and others. What was supposed to have been reborn in the new age was *bonae litterae*, 'good letters', in other words language, literature and learning. This was at any rate the opinion of the scholars and writers whose account of the great revival has come down to us, since artists (with the distinguished exception of Vasari) left few records of their views on the subject. It is important to keep in mind this bias in the surviving evidence.

The main language which was 'reborn' or 'revived' at this time was not Italian, but classical Latin. Medieval Latin was coming to be regarded as 'barbarous', in its vocabulary, its spelling (*michi* in place of the classical *mihi*), its syntax, and so on. 'Not only has no one spoken Latin correctly for many centuries', wrote the scholar Lorenzo Valla in the 1440s, 'but no one has even understood it properly when reading it.' In his day, however, it became the ambition of some scholars to write Latin like Cicero.

These scholars also revived the principal literary genres of ancient Rome; the epic, the comedy, the ode, the pastoral, and so on [46]. As early as the mid-fourteenth century, the great Tuscan poet-scholar Francesco Petrarca ('Petrarch') produced a Latin epic, the *Africa*, based on the life of the great Roman general Scipio Africanus. It was the first of many imitations of Virgil's *Aeneid*, in which heroic deeds were narrated according to a set of conventions including beginning in the middle (with later flash-backs), and alternating deeds done on earth with councils of the gods. Tasso's *Jerusalem Delivered* (1581), a story of the First Crusade, is at once one of the most deeply christian and profoundly classical of Renaissance epics. Tragedies were written in the melo-dramatic manner of Seneca, piling the stage with corpses, and comedies in the style of the ancient Roman playwrights Plautus and Terence, complete with heavy fathers, cunning servants, boastful soldiers and mistaken identities. The Latin

11

poetry of Renaissance Italy included odes in the manner of Horace, epigrams in the manner of Martial, and pastoral in the manner of Virgil's *Eclogues*, in which shepherds play their pipes in an Arcadian landscape and sing of their yearning for their loves. Ideas were frequently discussed in the form of dialogues inspired by those of ancient writers such as Plato and Cicero. Histories of Florence, Venice and other Italian states were modelled on Livy's history of Rome.

The fact that vernacular literature was taken less seriously than Latin – before 1500, at least – deserves emphasis. Although Petrarch is most appreciated today for his Italian love-lyrics, he would have preferred to have been remembered for his *Africa*. Paradoxically enough, it was classical Latin which was the language of innovation. There was a time-lag of more than a century between the first Renaissance comedies in Latin and their equivalents in Italian such as Ariosto's *Suppositi* (1509), and cardinal Bibbiena's *Calandria* (1513). Leonardo Bruni's Latin *History of the Florentine People* goes back to the early fifteenth century; the first Italian work in the same class, Francesco Guicciardini's *History of Italy*, was written more than a hundred years later [25, 29]. When contemporaries mentioned the revival of 'letters', they were generally referring not to literature in the modern sense so much as to what is known today as the rise of humanism.

'Humanism' is a somewhat elastic term, with different meanings for different people. The word *Humanismus* came into use in Germany in the early nineteenth century to refer to the traditional type of classical education, the value of which was beginning to be questioned, while Matthew Arnold seems to have been the first to use the term 'humanism' in English. As for 'humanist', the word originated in the fifteenth century as student slang for a university teacher of the 'humanities' (the *studia humanitatis*). This was an ancient Roman phrase to describe an academic package of five subjects in particular; grammar, rhetoric, poetry, ethics and history [5].

The reader may well be wondering what was particularly human about the humanities, defined in this way. They are so-called, wrote Leonardo Bruni, one of the leaders of the movement to revive these studies, because they 'perfect man'.

But why should these five subjects be regarded as perfecting man? The fundamental idea was that man differs from animals primarily by the ability to speak and therefore to distinguish right from wrong. Hence the fundamental subjects of study were those dealing with language (grammar and rhetoric), or with ethics; and both history and poetry were regarded as kinds of applied ethics, teaching students to follow good examples and avoid evil ones. The scholars of the period were not afraid to generalise about the 'human condition', as Poggio called it, or to compose orations, like Pico della Mirandola, on the 'Dignity of Man' – though this was not intended by Pico as a declaration of independence from God [27]. The basic assumptions of the humanists are neatly illustrated in a diagram from an early sixteenth-century work by the French humanist Charles de Bouelles (Plate 6). According to this diagram, there are four levels of existence. In ascending order they are to exist like a stone, to live like a plant, to feel like a horse and to understand like a man. There are four corresponding kinds of human being; the sluggard, the glutton, the vain person, and the scholar. In other words, humanity is perfectible, but only the humanist is truly human.

The diagram also implies that the life of contemplation is superior to the life of action. There was in fact no consensus on this issue. Leonardo Bruni, chancellor of the Florentine republic, suggested that a man could fulfil himself only as a citizen, while Marsilio Ficino, a philosopher who accepted the patronage of the Medici, preferred study and contemplation. Erasmus too protected his liberty to study and write and refused to be tied down by political commitments. Other humanists were torn between action and contemplation, like Sir Thomas More, who found the decision whether to become a councillor to Henry VIII (and later Lord Chancellor) a difficult one to take, or Montaigne, who broke off his studious retirement in his tower to become Mayor of Bordeaux at a time of civil war [70, 71].

It will be obvious that the studies most emphasised by the humanist movement did not include what we call 'science' ('natural philosophy' was a common term at the time). However, some leading humanists (Alberti, for example) were

13

interested in mathematics in particular. In any case, the recovery of the texts of ancient Greek and Roman writers on mathematics, medicine, astronomy, astrology and (not least) on magic was part of the humanist programme, and the classical texts were virtually indispensable for the future development of these studies. It may therefore be argued that there was a mathematical, a scientific and even a magical 'Renaissance' in the period [31, 32, 33]. In the cases of Brunelleschi and Leonardo da Vinci, the links between the arts and the Renaissance of mathematics are particularly obvious [18, 67].

In what sense was there a 'rise' of humanism in Italy between 1300 and 1600? Just as there were attempts to revive classical art and literature, an effort was made to imitate the educational system of ancient Rome. One of the pioneers of the new kind of education was Vittorino da Feltre, who ran a small boarding-school at Mantua from 1423 to 1446; another was Guarino da Verona [24, 28]. The new system involved teaching the students to speak and write as well as to read classical Latin, and it also meant an emphasis on the humanities at the expense of other subjects, notably logic. Logic had been central to the introductory arts course in medieval universities, but it was attacked by Petrarch, Valla and other humanists on the grounds that it was futile, mere quibbling or hair-splitting, and that it required the use of 'barbarous' (in other words, non-classical) technical terms like 'substance', 'accidents', 'quiddity' and so on.

In a few schools and in some Italian universities, notably in Florence (from 1396 onwards), and in Padua (from 1463), it was also possible to study classical Greek. Classical Athens was not yet such an object of admiration as classical Rome, but the Greek language did attract students. The first professors were refugees from the Byzantine Empire, which was falling piece by piece to the Turks long before the capture of Constantinople in 1453. Thanks to these refugees, some Italian scholars had the opportunity to read important Greek texts in the original language. Some of these texts were newly discovered, including the dialogues of Plato and the works of the mysterious 'Hermes Trismegistus' (believed to be an ancient Egyptian sage), which were translated by the Florentine philosopher Marsilio Ficino, whose admiration for Plato was so intense that he and his followers are often described as 'neoplatonists' [5, 39].

Other texts now studied in the original Greek, such as the New Testament and the works of Aristotle, had previously been known in Latin translations. However, the humanists discovered serious discrepancies between these translations (which had been made in some cases from Arabic translations from the Greek) and the original texts. It was because he had read Aristotle in the original Greek the sixteenth-century Italian philosopher Pietro Pomponazzi became convinced that St Thomas Aquinas had been wrong to suggest that Aristotle taught the immortality of the soul, and so to threaten the whole Thomist synthesis. Thus the quest for accurate translations gradually led to the discovery that the ideas of the admired ancients were more remote, more alien than had been thought.

According to the humanists, even classical Latin texts had long been misunderstood, when they had not been lost altogether. The rediscovery of manuscripts of the classics was an exciting event in the lives of scholars such as Petrarch and Coluccio Salutati (who recovered Cicero's letters between them) and Poggio Bracciolini (who found Cicero's speeches). However, it was found that different manuscripts of the same text contained different readings of key words, and techniques had to be developed for 'textual criticism', in other words the recovery of what the author had originally written before the chain of copyists distorted the message (83: ch. 12; 86].

Classical texts which had been known in the Middle Ages were given new interpretations. Roman law had been studied in Italian universities, notably Bologna, from the eleventh century onwards, but the humanists were the first to interpret the laws by placing them in the context of the culture and society of ancient Rome, which the study of classical literature and inscriptions was making more familiar to them. It was, for example, his knowledge of Roman history, and more especially of the history of the Latin language, which allowed the humanist Lorenzo Valla to demonstrate, in the middle of the fifteenth century, that the so-called 'Donation of Constantine', a document in which the emperor handed over

15

central Italy to the pope and his successors, had nothing to do with Constantine but was written several centuries later [41].

There were two apparently contradictory elements in the attitude to classical antiquity of the humanists and the artists who were associated with them. On the one hand, they were much more conscious of the distance between the classical past and the present than their medieval predecessors had been, and concerned with what they called the corruption of the language and the decline of the arts after the barbarians invaded Italy. On the other hand, they felt personally close to the great Romans. Petrarch wrote letters to Cicero and others, while Machiavelli described himself as conversing with the ancients. Both men believed that antiquity could be revived. Petrarch took a sympathetic interest in the attempted restoration of the Roman Republic, which lasted – within the city walls – from 1347 to 1354. Machiavelli argued passionately in his *Discourses on Livy* that ancient Roman political and military arrangements, such as the citizen militia, could and should be imitated by modern states [62, 68, 72].

To understand the revival of classical forms in architecture, say, or in the drama, or the enthusiasm for the discovery and editing of classical manuscripts, we need to see them as portions of a far more ambitious enterprise. It was nothing less than the restoration to life of ancient Rome. What could this mean? It is not always easy to decide whether the humanists were writing literally or metaphorically, or exactly how much of the past they wanted to bring back. However, the basic idea of revival was much more than a figure of speech. Like the ancients, many humanists believed in a cyclical interpretation of history, according to which one age could be a kind of recurrence or rerun of an older one. Some of them thought that they and their fellow-citizens could become 'new Romans' in the sense of speaking like the Romans, writing like them, thinking like them, and emulating their achievements, from the Colosseum and the *Aeneid* to the Roman Empire itself. This idea of a return to the past may have been, as suggested above, a myth, but it was a myth which some people not only believed but lived.

16

One of the key concepts of the humanists was that of 'imitation'; not so much the imitation of nature as that of great writers and artists. Today, this idea has come to sound strange. We have become accustomed to the idea that poems and paintings are expressions of the thoughts and feelings of creative individuals, and although we are aware that some artists do in fact imitate others, we are inclined to think of this as a sign of their lack of talent or an error on the part of people who have yet to 'find themselves' and develop their personal style. 'Imitation' has become a pejorative term. Writers and artists are anxious to emphasise their originality, spontaneity and independence, and to deny the 'influence' of their predecessors (let alone plagiarism, which has come to be regarded as the theft of someone else's intellectual property). In the Renaissance, on the other hand, writers and artists tended to suffer from the opposite anxiety. Although we tend to think of this period as an age of innovation and originality, the men who lived in it stressed their imitation of the best ancient models; the Pantheon, the Laocöon, Cicero, Virgil, Livy and so on [49].

This imitation was not slavish. To use a favourite metaphor of the time, it did not 'ape' the ancients. The aim was rather to assimilate the model, to make it one's own, and even if possible to surpass it. It was generally held that the 'moderns' had no hope of equalling the achievements of the ancients, let alone going beyond them, but this was itself a challenge. Michelangelo was able, as we have seen, to pass off one of his statues as a genuine antique. Alberti wrote a Latin comedy which was mistaken for a classical work. A sixteenth-century humanist, Carlo Sigonio, 'discovered' a lost work of Cicero's, which turned out to be a creation of his own.

How close imitations should be to their originals was a matter for controversy. The poet-scholar Angelo Poliziano was one of those who emphasised the need to keep some distance from classical models, however prestigious. 'Those who compose only on the basis of imitation strike me as parrots or magpies bringing out things they don't understand. Such writers lack strength and life' [49; ch. 8]. The sixteenth-century Venetian critic Pietro Bembo believed in imitating Cicero when writing in Latin, but he was also concerned to make Italian a dignified literary language, with the four-teenth-century Tuscan writers Petrarch and Boccaccio as the best models, the modern 'classics'. The growing sense of historical distance made imitation problematic. 'Whom did the ancients imitate?' some people were asking. Did imitation become inappropriate as times changed? Whether they liked it or not, Renaissance artists and writers were unable to imitate the ancients in more than a partial manner. For one thing, the products of antiquity had survived only piecemeal. In painting, as we have seen, and also in music, there were no products of antiquity to imitate. Painters and musicians were forced to be free. However, the lack of specific models in certain genres was a minor problem compared to the fundamental fact that the Italians of the Renaissance lived in a very different world from that of the ancients. Their economic, social and political system was very different from that of ancient Rome with its senators and slaves, its legion-aries and latifundia. In this situation the ideal of restoring ancient Rome to life could never be more than a dream. We have returned to the Renaissance myth of the Renaissance. In reality, Petrarch, Brunelleschi, Alberti, Valla, Mantegna, Ficino, and other scholars, writers and artists of the fourteenth and fifteenth centuries were in many ways distant from what they felt was close, ancient Rome, and close to what they treated as distant, the 'Middle Ages'. Although they rejected the recent past of 'Gothic' art, 'scholastic' philosophy, and 'barbarous' Latinity, they had been brought up in this late medieval culture and in many ways still belonged to it. Trained as they had been in Gothic script, for example, they found ancient Roman inscriptions difficult to read.

Rejecting the late Middle Ages they knew, the humanists sometimes mistook the earlier medieval period for the antiquity they admired so much. When, for example, the humanist Poggio devised the handwriting we call 'Renais-sance' or 'Italic', he thought he was following classical exemp-lars. In fact his paradigms came from the earlier, pre-Gothic Middle Ages. In similar fashion Brunelleschi took the Bap-tistery in Florence as a model for his architectural reforms, thinking that it was a classical temple, whereas it has turned out to be an example of the Tuscan Romanesque, probably built in the eighth century [22; 83: ch. 27].

The continuities with the Middle Ages are visible as late as the sixteenth century, even in the work of such exemplary 'Renaissance men' as Lodovico Ariosto and Baldassare Castiglione. Ariosto's most famous work is the narrative poem *Orlando Furioso* (1516). It bears the marks of Ariosto's study of classical epic, but even more obvious is its debt to medieval romance, notably to the Charlemagne cycle (Orlando is none other than the hero Roland). The poem is no ordinary romance of chivalry; it treats the medieval material too ironically for that. But it is no simple imitation of classical epic either. It could only have been written by someone who in a sense belonged to both traditions, and so to neither. Ironic detachment is the only possible stance for a man with a foot in both camps [46: part 2]. Again, Castiglione's well-known *Courtier* (1528), despite its references to ancient precedent, notably to Cicero's treatise on the perfect orator, is concerned to lay down the rules for playing a social role unknown in classical Athens or republican Rome but very well known in the Middle Ages. It may be described as a medieval courtesy-book rewritten under the influence of classical ideals of behaviour, or an adaptation of those ideals to fit a non-classical situation. Like Ariosto's poem, it could only have been written by someone with an intimate knowledge of both traditions, ancient and medieval.

One area in which the ambiguities and conflicts inherent in the humanist position became manifest was the writing of history. Leonardo Bruni and Lorenzo Valla were among the historians who wanted to write about the recent Italian past while following the model of Livy's history of Rome, including the model of Livy's language. Yet their subject-matter made this impossible; there was no classical Latin term for Lombardy, for the political factions of Guelf and Ghibelline, for Muslims, for cannon, and so on, because these objects and institutions had not existed in Roman times. It was not possible to pour all the new material into the classical mould. Giorgio Vasari wrote his *Lives* of painters, sculptors and architects in Italian, thus avoiding certain linguistic problems;but his work too reveals a tension between his admiration for artists and for antiquity. His borrowings from classical texts such as Cicero's account of the rise and fall of rhetoric cannot hide the fact that his enterprise had no parallel in classical times and that the reason it had no parallel was that the ruling class of Greece and Rome had not taken artists seriously.

However, the contradictions in the human position were most obvious when they discussed religion. They were, after all, Christians, not worshippers of the pagan gods. Petrarch, Alberti, Valla and Ficino were all clerics. Alberti and Valla were both in papal service, while the humanist Aeneas Silvius Piccolomini became pope Pius II. Petrarch, Valla and Ficino all wrote on theology, while Alberti designed churches and wrote the biography of a saint.

Individual creations of the period may sometimes imitate ancient models very closely, but their social and cultural context was very different and many works of the Renaissance are what have been called cultural 'hybrids', classical in some ways but christian in others [13]. An epic poem might be written in classical Latin on the model of Virgil's *Aeneid*, yet deal with the life of Christ. A humanist theologian might refer to churches as 'temples', to the Bible as 'oracles', or to Hell as the 'underworld', or entitle his treatise (as Ficino did) *Platonic Theology*. A Renaissance tomb might imitate a classical sarcophagus (complete with winged personifications of Victory), yet combine this with images of Christ or the Virgin Mary [19, 20]. This combination of classical and christian is difficult to interpret, as syncretism often is, because it may have been undertaken for such different reasons. After four hundred years, it is not easy to decide whether Ficino was dressing Platonism up as theology or dressing theology up as Platonism. Nineteenth-century historians, including Burckhardt, tended to present the humanists as essentially 'pagans', who paid no more than lip-service to Christianity. Today, on the other hand, scholars are more likely to argue that the lip-service was paid to paganism. The use of classical phrases in christian contexts may have been no more than an attempt to write 'pure' Latin, or even a learned game, like the painter Mantegna and his friends calling themselves by Roman titles such as 'consul' when they made an excursion to Lake Garda one day in 1464 to look for classical antiquities.

To say this is not to deny that there was some degree of tension between classical values and christian ones, or that contemporaries saw this, or that it worried them. A similar problem had arisen in early christian times. The Fathers of the Church belonged to two cultures, the traditional classical culture and the new christian one, and they tried, with more or less difficulty, to harmonise the two – Athens and Jerusalem. In the case of Jerome, the internal conflict was so acute that it expressed itself in dramatic form, in his dream of being dragged before the court of Christ and condemned for being 'a Ciceronian, not a Christian'.

The Fathers resolved this conflict by means of a compromise, expressed in picturesque fashion by Augustine in his image of the 'spoils of the Egyptians'. When the Israelites went out of Egypt, the Old Testament tells us, they took Egyptian treasure with them, and in a similar way whatever is valuable in the pagan classics may be appropriated by Christians and put to their own uses. In any case, some early Christians believed that the ancient Greeks had learned true doctrine (the so-called 'ancient theology') from the Jews. 'What else is Plato', wrote Eusebius in the fourth century, 'but Moses speaking Attic Greek?' [39].

This compromise appealed to the humanists, whose problem was of course the opposite one of reconciling traditional Christian culture with the rediscovered classics. A few scholars, such as the fifteenth-century Greek refugee Gemistos Pletho, may possibly have abandoned Christianity for the worship of the ancient gods, but most of them wanted to become ancient Romans without ceasing to be modern Christians. Their desire for harmony led them to interpretations of antiquity which now seem somewhat far-fetched, such as treating the *Aeneid* as an allegory of the soul's progress through life. However, every age tends to see the past in its own image, and we must not imagine that our own is an exception.

In the case of the visual arts, the meaning of the revival of ancient forms is hard to interpret because we usually lack evidence of the artist's intentions, but there are signs of attempts to reconcile antiquity with Christianity and of the use of early christian models. The circular plan of Bramante's Tempietto (Plate 2), for instance, is reminiscent not only of

21

pagan temples but also of a particular type of early christian church built to commemorate a martyrdom, and San Pietro in Montorio was built to mark the spot where St Peter was supposed to have been crucified [22: ch. 6]. In the case of Michelangelo, his poems leave no doubt of his desire to combine classical forms with christian meanings [69].

However thoroughgoing it was supposed to be, the revival of antiquity was not intended as a substitute for Christianity. To say this is, however, to blur the distinction between Renaissance and Middle Ages, since classical forms had been imitated (as its modern name implies), in the 'Romanesque' art of the tenth and eleventh centuries, while classical poets such as Virgil and Horace had been studied in medieval monasteries and universities. We should not see the Renaissance as a cultural 'revolution' in the sense of a sudden break with the past. It is more accurate to think of the movement as a gradual development, in which more and more individuals became more and more dissatisfied with elements of their late medieval culture, and more and more attracted to the classical past.

Why did this happen? This question is the most difficult of all, not because it is hard to imagine possible answers but because it is impossible to nail these answers down with precise evidence. Was the cult of antiquity a means to an end, a way of justifying the break with the recent past? Or were these people interested in the ancient world entirely for its own sake? To be plausible, any account of this collective attempt to revive ancient Greece and Rome must make sense of three factors; the geography of the movement, its chronology, and its sociology. Why should such a movement have arisen in north-central Italy? Why should it have gathered increasing momentum in the fourteenth, fifteenth and sixteenth centuries? And why should it have appealed in particular to urban patricians? Let us take these three questions in order.

It does not look like an accident that the revival of antiquity began in Italy, on the site of the original achievements – for it was Rome, not Greece, which was the main object of enthusiasm – Virgil rather than Homer, the Pantheon not the Parthenon. In a metaphorical sense, the humanists were discovering their ancestors, while some noble families claimed literal descent from ancient Romans. The remains of antiquity – coins, tombs, temples, amphitheatres and so on – were relatively familiar to Italians, including of course Italian artists. Indeed, it is difficult to decide whether the classical inspiration in eighth-, twelfth- or even fourteenth-century Italian art should be seen as survival or revival. When imitation of antiquity became more frequent, more thorough and more self-conscious, we speak of the 'Renaissance', but in Italy, unlike some other parts of Europe, the classical traditon had never been remote.

Chronology is more of a problem. If the remains of antiquity had so long been part of the Italian landscape (or, in the case of some classical texts, available in libraries in Verona and elsewhere), why should they have been taken so seriously only from the time of Petrarch onwards? The obvious answer to this question is that the example of antiquity must have come to seem more relevant to contemporary needs. So what had changed? The most conspicuous change was the rise of the north Italian city-state in the twelfth and thirteenth centuries, in other words the seizure of self-government by the towns [7]. The rise of these towns can be explained in economic terms, by the increasing trade between Europe and the Middle East. It is not difficult to see why their merchant oligarchies should have wished to be independent, and their location on the border between the dominions of the popes and the emperors made the achievement of independence a smoother process than it might otherwise have been. The ruling groups of these cities came to see themselves as 'consuls' or 'patricians'; their town councils as the equivalent of the 'Senate'; the city itself as a 'new Rome'. The process is particularly clear in the case of Florence in the early fifteenth century, when the threat from Milan helped make the Florentines, and their spokesman the humanist chancellor Leonardo Bruni, more conscious of who they were and of the values, such as 'liberty', which they were defending [25]. But this dramatc episode is part of a much longer story of a growing sense of affinity with the Romans, to be found in the towns of northern Italy from the twelfth century, if not before.

Attempting to explain the chronology of the Renaissance has raised the third question, that of its social basis. It is clear that the Renaissance was a minority movement. It was urban not rural, and the praises of the countryside flowed from the pens of individuals whose main residence was the house in town, not the country villa. The movement appealed to men rather than women, though some noblewomen were active as patrons. Isabella d'Este, for example, Marchioness of Mantua in the early sixteenth century, was an enthusiastic art collector who acquired works by such masters as Bellini, Perugino, Leonardo and Titian. A few women studied the classics for themselves and wrote letters and treatises in Latin, only to find, like Isotta Nogarola of Verona, that male humanists, like Guarino, refused to treat them on equal terms with men. Within the group of males living in towns, the revival of antiquity appealed to a minority, or more exactly to three minorities. There were the humanists, who tended to be professional men, teachers or notaries. There were the members of the ruling class, patricians, prelates or princes, who extended their patronage to the new forms of art and learning. There were also the artists, who were recruited in the main from the children of urban craftsmen and shopkeepers [6: ch. 3].

To what extent humanists and artists shared the same interests is far from clear. Some paintings, such as Botticelli's *Calumny* (Plate 3), or his *Primavera*, presuppose a knowledge of ancient literature which the artist, who left school at thirteen, is unlikely to have possessed, and it has been suggested that the 'programme' of the latter painting must have come from a humanist adviser such as Ficino or Poliziano, who are likely to have been acquaintances if not friends of Botticelli. On the other hand, it is far from clear whether most humanists understood the passionate interest shown by Brunelleschi, Donatello and other artists in the formal aspects of ancient architecture and sculpture. Alberti, who was a friend of Brunelleschi, Donatello and the painter Masaccio, and wrote plays and dialogues as well as designing buildings, was one of the few men to bridge the gap between these two cultures. Even Leonardo da Vinci, despite the breadth of his interests, remained on one side of the divide [67]. The 'uni-

24

versal man' who could master everything was a contemporary ideal, but it is difficult to find many people who incarnated it, even in an age when the pressure to specialise was much less than it is today.

In short, the revival of antiquity did not have the same meaning for every social group. It meant something different in Florence, Rome, Venice and so on. This point becomes particularly obvious if we consider the history of the movement over time. In the fourteenth century, we see an increasing interest in the classical past on the part of a handful of enthusiasts, notably Petrarch, who, far from being 'one of the first truly modern men', belonged to late medieval culture, even if he was coming to reject some aspects of it. By the sixteenth century, however, thanks in part to the more rapid diffusion of ideas and other intellectual changes facilitated by that new invention, printing, a good deal more of classical culture had been assimilated, and the tiny group of enthusiasts had turned into a large one, including a considerable number of teachers. Indeed, it was now possible to be introduced to many of these ideas and ideals at school. It was becoming fashionable for noblemen – and women – to discuss the ideas of Plato (as they are shown doing in Castiglione's *Courtier*), to collect classical statues, to commission portraits of themselves, or to have town houses and country villas built in the 'ancient' style.

This enlargement in the public for the Renaissance was not the only significant development in the fifteenth and sixteenth centuries. There were other changes too. The best-known account of the different phases of the movement is the one given by the artist-historian Giorgio Vasari, who distinguished three periods in the arts; early, middle and what is now known as 'High' Renaissance. Vasari writes as if the achievements of each age surpassed those of the one before, while the goal remained the same. It may be argued, however, that the aims of artists and writers gradually changed during the period. In architecture and literature alike, a concern to create according to ancient principles gave way in many cases to the ideal of following the 'rules' encoded in ancient examples. One might say (exaggerating a little for the sake of clarity), that a movement which had once seemed

25

subversive (to some scholastic philosophers at least) had, by the year 1500 or thereabouts, become part of the establishment. It had been institutionalised, routinised, incorporated into tradition, so that historians have good reason to describe a whole period in Italian history as that of the Renaissance.

Outside Italy, however, the revival of antiquity was still a novelty; the movement had not lost its power to shock. It is to what was happening outside Italy that we must now turn our attention.

3 The Renaissance Abroad: or the Uses of Italy

It should by now be clear that the imitation of antiquity, the distinctive trait of the Renaissance, was no simple process. It was problematic and it was seen at the time to be problematic. The same has to be said of the imitation of Italian culture in other countries, as this section will try to show.

It is customary to introduce this topic with an account of the activities of Italians abroad and of foreign visitors to Italy, and there is nothing wrong in that. However, students of the subject have long been dissatisfied with the traditional account of the 'diffusion' or 'reception' of the Renaissance abroad, an account which carries the misleading implication that while the Italians were active, creative and innovatory, the rest of Europe was passive, a mere recipient of 'influence' or, to use another metaphor beloved by historians, a 'borrower', eternally in debt to Italy.

For one thing, the position of the rest of Italy relative to Tuscany, and more especially to Florence, was not unlike that of other European countries. The new style in architecture, for example, appeared in Venice only after a certain time-lag, and it had to be modified before it was accepted. Again, it is not the case that Italy was the only seat of cultural innovation. It was not in Tuscany but at the papal court of Avignon that Petrarch had some of his most important experiences, made some of his most significant friendships, and wrote some of his most famous poems [72]. It was in the Netherlands that a new technique of oil painting was developed in the early fifteenth century by Jan van Eyck, Roger van de Weyden, and others, and this technique was influential in Italy, where paintings by Flemish masters were much appreciated. In music, the Netherlands was recognised as pre-eminent, even by Italians; the Donatello of music, as one Italian writer put it, was Ockeghem, and its Michelangelo was Josquin des Près [54]. Major artists and writers such as Holbein and Dürer, Erasmus and Montaigne, Shakespeare and Cervantes were inspired by Italian models, but not by these alone, and in any case they did not follow their models slavishly. In other words, the traditional account of the reception of the Renaissance is misguided. But what can we put in its place?

Historians and literary critics alike have recently been undermining the dichotomy between cultural 'production' and 'consumption', and emphasising the way in which we all modify what we acquire and suit it to our needs. So at this point it may be worth asking what the uses of Italy were for artists, writers and scholars from other parts of Europe in the fifteenth and sixteenth centuries, thus switching attention from what one might call 'supply' to 'demand' and looking not such much at what was borrowed (let alone from whom), as at the process by which it was assimilated, absorbed, reworked, domesticated, transformed. In other words, this version of the 'reception' of the Renaissance outside Italy (to use the traditional term), will attempt to take account of what has come to be known as 'reception theory', the attempt by some students of literature to replace the simple idea of 'influence' by the more subtle one of a process of creative misinterpretation. So when we look at the Italians abroad, we need to ask not only who went where, at what time, and for what purpose, but also what kind of reception (in yet another sense of the term), they received.

Italian humanists and artists seem to have gone abroad in two separate waves. The humanists went first. Although Petrarch had made visits to the Netherlands and Paris in the fourteenth century, the real humanist brain drain seems to have taken place between the 1430s and the 1520s, with the late fifteenth century as the period in which humanist emigration was at its height. Italian scholars went to France, to Hungary, to England, to Spain, to Poland, to Portugal. Few of those who left were in the top flight; indeed, one is entitled to suspect that some of them migrated because they were not able to find a good position at home. As for the

28

artists, a rather more distinguished group, most of them ᵥ
abroad about a generation later than the humanists, so
the movement was at its height in their case in the early
sixteenth century. As in the case of the humanists, the largest
cluster of émigrés was to be found in France, among them
the painters Rosso and Primaticcio, the goldsmith Benvenuto
Cellini, the architect Sebastiano Serlio, and Leonardo da
Vinci, all invited by François I, one of the great patrons of
the Northern Renaissance [38].

Why did they go abroad? Today, the decision to travel, or
even to work abroad may be taken relatively lightly, but in
those days the difficulties and dangers of travelling as well
as the pain of exile must have made the decision a difficult
one in most cases. Some artists and humanists left Italy for
reasons which had little to do with the Renaissance. A few
of them went on diplomatic missions, like Aeneas Sylvius
Piccolomini (later pope Pius II) in Central Europe, or Baldassare Castiglione, who ended his life as papal nuncio in
Spain. Others were exiles for political or other reasons.
Filippo 'Callimaco' for example (nicknamed after an ancient
Greek scholar-poet), a man who made an important contribution to the development of humanism in Poland, had
had to leave Italy in a hurry after the conspiracy in which
he had been involved was unsuccessful. The religious exiles
are well known. Lelio and Fausto Sozzini, for example, were
scholars from Siena who found it wise to leave Italy in the
mid-sixteenth century to escape the inquisition, because they
did not believe in the doctrine of the Trinity (it is after
them that rejection of this doctrine came to be known ás
'Socinianism'). The Sozzinis and other exiles such as Peter
Martyr Vermigli, who found refuge in Oxford, belong to the
category of Italian humanists abroad no less than to that of
heretics. There were also exiles for personal reasons. Giorgio
Vasari, who rarely misses an opportunity to tell a good story,
informs us that the sculptor Pietro Torrigiani of Florence had
to leave town after a quarrel in which he broke Michelangelo's
nose. Had it not been for that brawl, the Henry VII chapel
at Westminster might lack its fine Renaissance tomb. In the
history of the Renaissance, as in history in general, one must
never forget the importance of unintended consequences.

It is of course these consequences which make the visits of historical interest. Consequences such as the formal or informal instruction given by the visitors in Greek, or rhetoric, or poetry, or sculpture, or simply the encouragement to break with local tradition. At a chance meeting in Granada, in southern Spain, in 1526, Andrea Navagero, the Venetian ambassador, who was also a well-known poet, persuaded the Catalan Juan Boscán to write poems in the Italian manner.

The cultural consequences of these visits were not always unintended. Some of the Italians went abroad because they had been invited, by royal patrons such as François I, or by local aristocrats with literary or artistic interests, like Jan Zamojski, the chancellor of Poland in the later sixteenth century, who employed an Italian architect to design his new town, called Zamość after its founder [37]. The patrons themselves might be Italians living abroad in colonies of merchants in cities such as Bruges or Lyons. Italian princesses were also cultural intermediaries, the obvious examples being Beatrice of Aragon, wife of Mátyás of Hungary, Bona Sforza of Milan, who married King Zygmunt of Poland, and Catherine de'Medici of Florence, wife and widow of Henri II of France. Even soldiers might take an interest in the art patronage; the painter Masolino was invited to Hungary by a Tuscan mercenary captain, Pippo Spano.

What were the local responses to these Italian migrants, their ideas and their skills? Some of them received an extremely warm welcome abroad. The Lombard humanist Pietro Martire d'Anghiera, for example, has left a famous account of his visit to the university of Salamanca in 1488, when he delivered a lecture on the poet Juvenal. There were so many people in the audience that he could not get into the lecture-room until the beadle had cleared a passage with his staff, and when he had given his lecture, the visitor was carried off in triumph, so he tells us, like a victor at the Olympic games. Perhaps he was exaggerating the enthusiasm. Pietro Martire was, after all, a professional rhetorician. But he had had an experience worth describing to his patron. There were similar crowds, including members of the general public as well as students and teachers, to hear Girolamo Aleandro lecture on the Latin poet Ausonius in Paris in 1511.

Other Italian humanists abroad seem to have had a rather cooler reception, if their itinerant careers are anything to go by. Girolamo Balbo began by teaching in Paris, but moved on to the Netherlands, Germany and Bohemia, while Jacopo Publicio was active in Germany and Switzerland before settling in Portugal. All the same, comparatively minor figures, who had never been well known in Italy, had the chance of becoming important people abroad, like Antonio Bonfini, who was a schoolmaster in the small town of Recanati before becoming court historian to Mátyás of Hungary. In his time, the late fifteenth century, Italian humanists were in particularly high demand because there was a local interest in classical literature and learning without native humanists to cater for it. A few years later, when a new generation had been trained in humanism, it would be possible to do without these expatriates.

One sign of indigenous interest in Renaissance culture in many parts of Europe is the traffic in the other direction. Of course the many visitors to Italy went for a number of different reasons. They did not all go to meet scholars or look at paintings or to see the ruins of ancient Rome. As in the Middle Ages, diplomats, clerics, soldiers, merchants and pilgrims continued to make their way to Italy. Among the visitors with interests in Italian culture the largest group was that of the students, bound for two universities in particular, Padua and Bologna, to study two subjects, law and medicine. Law and medicine were not part of the *studia humanitatis*. They were gradually transformed under the influence of humanism, but we cannot assume that all the teachers approved of these innovations, still less that the students (or their fathers, who paid for them) associated Italy with novelty.

After these qualifications have been made, it is still possible to point to some well-documented visits to Italy which were made for what might be called good Renaissance reasons. Some artists went to Italy to study the new style of painting or the remains of classical sculpture and architecture. Albrecht Dürer, for example, was in Venice in 1505–6 and met Giovanni Bellini (whom he described as 'still the best in painting'), and other artists [65]. The Netherlander Jan van Scorel was in Italy in the 1520s, and his pupil Maarten van Heemskerck

31

was in Rome in the 1530s, where he met Vasari as well as sketching ancient and modern buildings (Plate 8). The French architect Philibert de l'Orme was also in Rome in the 1530s.

Scholars went to Italy to learn about texts and approaches unavailable at home. The two best-known scientists, or natural philosophers, of the sixteenth century are probably Copernicus and Vesalius. Copernicus, who came from Poland, studied Greek, mathematics and astronomy at the universities of Bologna, Padua and Ferrara at the end of the fifteenth century, studies which left many traces on his major work, *On the Revolutions of the Heavenly Orbs* (1543), which argued that the sun was at the centre of the universe [3]. Vesalius, who came from Flanders, went to the university of Padua to study medicine, including anatomy, the subject of his famous book *On the Fabric of the Human Body*, also published in 1543. Another clear example of a scholar or writer visiting Italy for the sake of the new learning is that of Sir Thomas Hoby, a gentleman from Herefordshire best known for his English version of Castiglione's *Courtier*. Hoby's journal reveals that he went to Padua in 1548 to study Italian and 'humanitie', although he also attended lectures on logic and Roman law. The Netherlander Justus Lipsius, one of the greatest scholars of the second half of the sixteenth century, went to Rome in 1567 in the retinue of his patron cardinal Granvelle in order to meet classical scholars, such as Carlo Sigonio, and to study the ancient world at first hand [46]. The French historian Jacques-Auguste de Thou recorded his passion to see Italy in his autobiography. On arrival in 1573 he bought Greek texts in Venice and visited the picture collection at Mantua which had been formed by Isabella d'Este. He also met Vasari and Sigonio. A few years later, in 1580–1, it was the turn of Montaigne to visit Italy, where he admired the ruins of ancient Rome and looked at classical manuscripts in the Vatican Library.

In many other cases, however, it was once again the unintended consequences which were important; the discovery of antiquity or the Renaissance by visitors who were not in search of them. For example, the German nobleman Ulrich von Hutten went to Italy to study law, but while he was there discovered the attractions of classical literature, in particular the satirical dialogues of Lucian, which served him as a model when he became involved in the polemics of the Reformation. Sir Thomas Wyatt discovered Italian poetry when he was on a diplomatic mission (as Geoffrey Chaucer had done long before in similar circumstances), and the example of Petrarch inspired his own poems. Wyatt's Spanish contemporary Garcilaso de la Vega met the poets Luigi Tansillo and Bernardo Tasso (the father of the more famous Torquato Tasso) in Naples, where he had been banished for a misdemeanour. Like his friend Boscán after his meeting with Navagero, Garcilaso wrote in a more Italian manner thereafter.

Of course the movement of individuals is not the whole story of the spread of the Renaissance. There was also the movement of paintings and statues, like the works of art which François I of France, one of the great patrons of the Renaissance, ordered from Florence [38]. There was the movement of books, the original texts and the translations of Petrarch's poems, Machiavelli's political works, the illustrated treatise on architecture by Sebastiano Serlio of Bologna (a pupil of Bramante who moved to France in the 1540s) and so on. The development of printing in the later fifteenth century had important effects on the Renaissance movement, as I shall try to show later in this section.

In some ways, the reception of books (translations in particular) is easier to analyse than the more elusive personal relationships discussed so far. It is possible to discover how much was translated, what was selected, what kinds of people made the translations and most important of all, it is possible to chart the popularity of particular texts and to study in detail the changes made by the translators. The less faithful the translations, the more valuable the evidence they offer of the process by which Italian texts (and in some cases also images) were adapted to the needs of foreign readers. The reception of the Renaissance – as of any alien system of values – was necessarily linked to its perception, and perception is of course shaped by schemata. In the sixteenth century, Italy was seen by foreigners as an exotic country, the opposite of the perceiver's own culture. Translations help document the process of the domestication of this dangerously attractive or attractively dangerous alien. The Italy which the non-Italians imitated was to some extent their creation, shaped by their needs and desires, just as the antiquity which both they and the Italians aspired to imitate was a construction of their own.

Two examples may serve to illustrate this general process. The first is the reception of Italian architecture abroad, while the second, still more specific, is that of reactions outside Italy to Castiglione's *Courtier*. Architecture seems especially relevant to the theme of 'the uses of Italy' because it is functional as well as decorative; because it obviously needs to be adapted to the local environment; and finally, because it is a collective art in which craftsmen as well as architects played a part. There were therefore many obstacles to any smooth diffusion abroad of designs made in Italy, despite the existence of pattern-books like the treatise by Serlio already mentioned, or Andrea Palladio's *Four Books of Architecture* (1570), books which were available in several European languages and could be studied by architects and, equally important in an age when master craftsmen were still responsible for most buildings, by their patrons. Even within Italy, local circumstances encouraged regional variation, so that the architecture of the Lombard or Venetian Renaissance was in many ways different from the Tuscan. These regional differences were in a sense 'exported'. The Hungarians imitated the Tuscans, but French architecture tended to follow the Lombard model and German architecture the Venetian.

Italian Renaissance architecture has been described as spreading not as a 'total configuration' but in fragments [34]. We might reasonably speak of 'bricolage', that is, of the incorporation of new Italian elements into traditional local structures, particularly in the first phase of reception. In France in the early sixteenth century, for example, Italian decoration had more of an appeal than Italian plans. In the case of the castle of Chambord, for instance, built for François I, the round towers are obviously traditional and only the architectural details are distinctively new. Local stone was used because it was cheaper and also (as Philibert de l'Orme observed) more suitable to the climate [35]. However, the material used necessarily affects the form. The architecture of Renaissance Italy was gradually acclimatised.

34

A Northern Artist in Rome: Martin van Heemskerck.

2. The High Renaissance: Bramante's Tempietto.

3. Antiquity Reconstructed: Botticelli's version of the *Calumny* of Apelles.

Antiquity Reconstructed II: Michaelangelo's Bacchus.

5. A Classical Paradigm: the Pantheon in Rome.

6. A Humanist View of the World: Bovillus.

In England too the imitation of Serlio, say, by the Elizabethan Robert Smythson, or of Palladio, by Inigo Jones, also involved modification for practical reasons as well as to express the architect's own ideas. The modifications may not always have gone far enough, and caustic remarks have often been made about the draughty porticos of English country houses which follow a classical design created for a Mediterranean climate. However, Sir Henry Wotton, in his *Elements of Architecture* (1624), showed himself to be well aware of the problem of draughts, and of the importance of items like chimneys and steep roofs, which were more important in England than in Italy.

The implication is not that Italian designs were modified for utilitarian reasons alone. To say this would be to adopt precisely the crude functionalism I have been trying to avoid. The modifications came about for a variety of reasons. Some were obviously intentional, others less so. In some cases, the divergences from Italian models were the result of the employment of local craftsmen who had their own traditions and were unable or unwilling to understand exactly what was being asked of them. Chambord, for example, designed for François I by an Italian architect, Domenico da Cortona, was actually built by French masons. The new town of Zamość in Poland was planned by an Italian, Morando, but the plans were once again carried out by local craftsmen. A spectacularly obvious example of the conflict and interpenetration of local traditions and Italian models can be seen in the architecture of the Renaissance in Spain, where in the south at least, the craft traditions of Islam were still strong.

On occasion it was the patron (who was still very much in control) who demanded modifications to Italian designs for symbolic reasons rather than utilitarian considerations. At the end of the fifteenth century, Tsar Ivan III of Russia asked an Italian, Aristotile Fioravanti, to design the cathedral of St Michael's at the Kremlin, but he required Fioravanti to follow the plan of the twelfth-century cathedral at Vladimir. The tsar's ambivalent attitude to the west is an extreme case of a not uncommon reaction to Italian culture. For a variety of reasons, then, what we find is not the simple export of Italian models abroad but their reconstruction, and the development of hybrid forms which need to be described in terms of misunderstanding (from the Italian point of view), or of creative adaptation. As a printed guide to action, to the construction of the self, Castiglione's *Courtier* has a status not unlike that of the architectural treatises of Serlio and Palladio. The diffusion, translation and imitation of this book has a good deal to tell us about the adoption and the assimilation of the Italian courtly ideal.

Castiglione's dialogue was published for the first time in 1528 and it was soon translated into Spanish and French and a little later, in 1561, into English. The Spanish translator was Juan Boscán and the English translator Thomas Hoby; their enthusiasm for Italian culture has already been discussed. Hoby claimed to have attempted, as he put it, 'to follow the very meaning and words of the author, without being misled by fantasy, or leaving out any parcel one or other'. However, at this time the English language lacked precise equivalents for some of Castiglione's key concepts, forcing Hoby to coin new terms. *Cortegiania* itself, which we might render today as 'courtiership', was paraphrased as 'the trade and manner of courtiers'. The famous concept of *sprezzatura*, a sort of careless grace, was rendered either by 'disgracing' or by 'recklessness'. It is not clear – to me at least – why Hoby did not use the word 'negligence' which Chaucer had used before him and which corresponds to the *negligentia* of Castiglione's own model, the ancient Roman Cicero. The point I wish to emphasise, though, is that the lack of English equivalents for Castiglione's keywords suggests that the diffusion of his ideas could not be smooth, despite the fact that the court as an institution was familiar enough in England, France, Spain and elsewhere.

Similar points could be made about the French and Spanish translations. Still more revealing, however, because it is still further from the original, is the Polish version of the *Courtier*, the *Dworzanin Polski*, published in 1566 by Lukasz Górnicki. It is not so much a translation as a transposition. The setting, for example, is moved from the court of Urbino in 1508 to that of Cracow in 1550, and the parts are all taken by Polish noblemen, women being eliminated on the grounds that they are not learned enough – in Poland – to take part in such conversations. Górnicki also declares that he is going to leave out Castiglione's discussion of the arts of painting and sculpture because 'we don't know about them here'. The controversies over the best form of Italian to speak and write are translated into comparisons between the different Slav languages.

In the strict sense of the term the *Dworzanin Polski* is an unreliable translation. However, given the views on imitation expressed in the *Courtier* itself – the idea that if we imitate the ancients we do not imitate them, because they did not imitate anyone – it might be argued that Górnicki was a more faithful translator than Hoby (say), precisely because he was less faithful. He was doing his best to translate Italian culture into Polish terms. His elimination of women was not arbitrary but expressed the gulf between the two cultures. It serves as a useful reminder of the social obstacles (no less than linguistic or climatic ones) to any simple diffusion of Italian values abroad.

So do the foreign attacks on Castiglione or on the young men who aspired to behave like his characters. They express an anti-Italian backlash, a hostility to what one is tempted to call Italian cultural imperialism, disguised as a defence of sincerity. The English poet John Marston, for example, satirised 'the absolute Castilio' and his 'ceremonious compliment'. In France, Castiglione was associated with dissimulation and with the 'corruption' of the French language by Italian words, a process which irritated the critics into coining such new terms as 'italianization'. There were similar attacks on Machiavelli, who was also associated with dissimulation and suspected of 'atheism' into the bargain; as the figure of 'Machiavel' explains in the prologue to Christopher Marlowe's *The Jew of Malta* (*c*.1591),

I count religion but a childish toy,
And hold there is no sin but ignorance.

This hostile reaction to Machiavelli, Castiglione and other writers was not merely anti-Italian; it was also anti-Catholic or, in the language of the day, 'anti-Papist'. One obstacle to the smooth diffusion of the Italian Renaissance abroad was the Reformation.

37

There is a common view that the major difference between the Renaissance north of the Alps and the movement in Italy itself was the rise of 'christian humanism', associated with Erasmus in particular. This view rests on the assumption – a false assumption, as suggested in section 2 above – that Italy was full of 'pagan' humanists, to whom the northerners can be contrasted. The leaders of the Italian movement were concerned with divinity as well as with the humanities, and they made a conscious effort to harmonise their devotion to antiquity with their Christianity, just as some of the Fathers of the Church had done. Indeed, they may reasonably be described as devoted to two antiquities, that of the Fathers as well as that of the classics [30]. North of the Alps the humanist movement was even more concerned with sacred studies [39; 60: ch. 14]. This was not because the northerners were better Christians; the difference was partly a result of the different institutional base of the movement (more closely associated with universities and even monasteries than had been the case in Italy), and partly a result of the timing, which coincided with the movement for the reform of the Church, before as well as after Martin Luther.

The model northern humanist is of course Erasmus, who lived from about 1466 to 1536 [16]. Erasmus was certainly interested in the classics, but in his thirties he turned to more christian studies. He spent a good deal of time on the textual criticism and translation of the Bible (going back to the original Greek version of the New Testament), and he also edited some of the Fathers of the Church, including Jerome and Origen. In some of his own writings he tried, like them, to harmonise christian with classical ideas. In one dialogue, *The Godly Feast* (1522), one speaker describes Cicero as 'divinely inspired', while another refers to the christian sentiments of Socrates, leading a third to declare that he 'can hardly help exclaiming, St Socrates, pray for us!'. However, tension remained, as a still more famous dialogue of Erasmus reveals. This is the *Ciceronianus* (1528), the title of which recalls Jerome's guilty dream. The protagonist of the dialogue, a certain Nosoponus, wants to write Latin exactly like Cicero. Another speaker objects that this would be impossible without bringing back the Rome of Cicero, thus underlining the paradox of imitation (by imitating the ancients in a changed world, we are not imitating them), and illustrating the Renaissance sense of the past, the new sensitivity to anachronism [49]. However, the main theme of the dialogue is that Cicero should not be imitated because he was a pagan. One speaker criticises the Latin epic on the Nativity written by the Italian poet Jacopo Sannazzaro on the grounds that he should have treated a sacred subject in a less classicising, less virgilian manner. The story is told of a sermon before Julius II which compared the pope to the pagan god Jupiter. The idea of Italian pagan humanism goes back at least as far as Erasmus. All the same, it is based on a misunderstanding and on misinformation. Recent research on preaching in the pope's chapel has failed to discover the sermon to which Erasmus objected.

The early sixteenth century was the most important moment of the interaction between the humanist movement and religious studies. It was in 1508 that a 'trilingual' college was founded in Alcalá, in Spain, to study the three languages of the Bible: Hebrew, Greek and Latin [43]. The Spanish humanist Juan Luis Vives edited Augustine and advocated the study in schools of early christian rather than pagan writers. In France, the theologian Jacques Lefêvre d'Etaples learned Greek to study the New Testament and the neo-platonic writers in the original language. In Germany, the great Hebrew scholar Johan Reuchlin was one of a group of humanists with theological interests. In London, Erasmus's friend John Colet put early christian writers such as Lactantius and the poet Juvencus on to the syllabus of his new school at St Paul's [60: ch. 15]. In Cambridge, the Professor of Greek, John Cheke, translated the great preacher John Chrysostom, bishop of Constantinople, as well as the ancient Greek tragedian Euripides.

The association between humanism and theology was at its height in the first two decades of the sixteenth century, before the excommunication of Luther and his conflict with Erasmus, but it did not disappear thereafter. What we see might be better described as the adaptation to new circumstances of humanist ideas and humanist skills. When humanism was defined, as it used to be, in terms of the 'dignity of man', Luther was seen as an anti-humanist because (unlike Erasmus) he did not believe in free will. However, he was no enemy of humanism in the sense of the *studia humanitatis*. He had had a classical education himself and he was sympathetic to the scholarly revival of ancient learning, which he believed to have been encouraged by God as a preparation for the reform of the Church. He supported Philip Melanchthon in his efforts to give the university of Wittenberg a humanist syllabus.

Zwingli was even closer to the humanists than Luther was, and believed that some of the virtuous pagans, such as Socrates, had been saved. Calvin was more ambivalent; he was suspicious of what he called *les sciences humaines* – in other words, the humanities – as 'vain curiosity'. However, he had studied them in his youth and edited a text by the Roman philosopher Seneca, and even in his maturity he did not reject Cicero and Plato altogether.

In Catholic Europe too the association between religious studies and the humanist movement outlasted the Reformation. It even outlasted the Council of Trent, although the humanists suffered a major defeat at the Council, in the early 1560s, in their attempts to replace the Vulgate, the official Latin version of the Bible, with a new translation from the original Greek and Hebrew. The notorious Index of Prohibited Books, which was made official by the Council of Trent, included the works of Erasmus, which was another defeat for the humanists. On the other hand, it did exempt classical literature, which remained an important part of the syllabus in the Catholic grammar schools, those of the Jesuits in particular. It is commonly said that the Jesuits supported the letter but not the spirit of humanism; but this interpretation depends to a large extent on the discredited view that 'real' humanists were essentially pagan or worldly. The Jesuit adaptation of the classical tradition to the needs of sixteenth-century Catholic boys differed in details but not in fundamentals from earlier attempts by Erasmus and Colet. It was not even so very different from the curricula devised by early humanist schoolmasters such as Vittorino da Feltre and Guarino da Verona. The main difference between humanist teachers and Jesuit teachers was that the first group rejected medieval philosophy while the second accepted it [60: ch. 16]. Just as some of the clergy tried to combine the techniques of humanism with those of medieval philosophy, so we find nobles attempting to fuse humanism with the attitudes and values of a military aristocracy, so that historians have had to invent hybrid terms like 'learned chivalry' or 'chivalric humanism' to describe the combination, whether in the courts of northern Italy (such as Ariosto's Ferrara), in fifteenth-century Burgundy, or in England under the Tudors [44].Count Baldassare Castiglione, the author of *The Courtier*, and Sir Philip Sidney preached and practised not only the new values associated with the Renaissance but also the traditional virtues of medieval knights – skill in warfare, chivalry and courtesy. The combination of old and new is particularly striking in the 'Accession Day Tilts' in the reign of Queen Elizabeth, in which knights, including Sidney, decorated their equipment with Renaissance devices, but fought in late medieval style, thus enacting the chivalric humanism which found its literary expression in the *Faerie Queene* [40].

One example after another prompts the generalisation that (like many other attempts at reform or renewal), the humanist movement became less radical and less distinctive as it became more successful. The history of political thought would seem to confirm this conclusion. The humanist movement grew up in the environment of the city-states of north and central Italy, shaping it and being shaped by it. Indeed, one scholar has argued that it was in the course of the Florentine 'struggle for liberty' against the duke of Milan around the year 1400 that the citizens turned to, or became conscious of, the specifically Renaissance values expressed by their chancellor, the humanist Leonardo Bruni [25; cf. 26, 42]. The state most closely associated with humanism, Florence, remained a republic in name at least, until 1530, although the writings of Machiavelli and Guicciardini suggest that the old confidence in reason and in man was shattered when the Florentines proved unable to resist the forces of Charles VIII of France, who invaded Italy in 1494 [29]. In Florence and in other republics, notably Venice and Genoa (which retained this form of government until the late eighteenth century), it was not difficult for the ruling class, and

41

the humanists associated with it, to identify with the men who had governed the ancient republics of Athens and Rome, and especially with Cicero, who combined the roles of politician, orator and philosopher. This humanist republicanism or 'civic humanism', as it is often called, had a certain appeal in some of the free cities of Germany and Switzerland. This was true of sixteenth-century Basel, for example, or of Nuremberg, where the town council included such men as Wilibald Pirckheimer, who was a friend of Dürer and a translator of Greek classics such as Plutarch and Lucian. Erasmus, who came from Rotterdam, one of the more or less independent cities of the Netherlands, was sympathetic to republics and often critical of princes who, he says, are rightly compared to eagles because that bird is greedy, rapacious and blood-thirsty (he may well have been thinking of the emperor Maximilian and his recent attempts to squeeze more taxes out of the Low Countries).

Elsewhere in Europe, on the other hand, monarchy was the norm, and the examples of classical or modern Italian republics had little pertinence. This was the world of the so-called 'Renaissance prince'. The term is a convenient one but unfortunately it is also somewhat ambiguous. If historians describe the emperor Charles V, for example, or François I, or Henry VIII in this way, they may mean that these princes took an interest in humanism or the arts, or that they governed in a new way (perhaps connected to the cultural changes of the time), or simply that they lived in the period which we call 'the Renaissance' in a rather vague sense. All three rulers took an interest in the new movements in art. Charles commissioned paintings from Titian, Henry VIII employed Holbein, while François, as we have seen, called Italian artists to court and built grandly at Chambord and Fontainebleau. The king's patronage of scholars, notably his foundation of the 'royal lecturers' in Greek and Hebrew, was extremely important in the establishment of humanism in France [38]. However, historians have become rather sceptical of the traditional assertion that these monarchs governed in a new, 'Renaissance' way, and tend to emphasise the survival of late medieval traditions of administration.

The essential relation between politics and the spread of

the Renaissance is one of a rather different kind. The political culture of northern Europe helped to determine what was taken from the classical tradition or from contemporary Italy, and also how it was interpreted. For example, it was its relevance to the societies across the Alps as well as its own literary merits which made Castiglione's *Courtier* so popular outside Italy. Although Machiavelli served the Florentine Republic, and wrote his "Discourses' on the early history of Rome for the instruction of his fellow-citizens in particular, outside Italy he was best known – or most notorious – for his little book of advice to princes. Thomas More may have been inspired to write his *Utopia* by the example of Plato's *Republic*, but it was the problems of the kingdom of England under Henry VIII with which he was professionally concerned [42, 71]. Erasmus too, whatever he thought of eagles, wrote a book on *The Education of a Christian Prince* for the benefit of the young emperor Charles V, telling him, among other things, that if he found he could not rule without injustice or the destruction of religion he should resign. Erasmus may well have had a classical precedent in mind, that of the Roman emperior Diocletian. However, his suggestion was to become more topical than he realised. In the year 1555 Charles did resign, following a civil war in his empire in which religious issues – Protestantism versus Catholicism – played an important part. One wonders whether the emperor was thinking of the advice given him by Erasmus forty years earlier.

Charles's court preacher, the Spanish friar Antonio de Guevara, was also involved in the humanist movement, and he turned his admonitions into the form of a treatise called *The Dial of Princes*, which drew heavily on the Roman moralist Seneca and held up before Charles the example of the emperor Marcus Aurelius. Guevara's work, which was often reprinted and translated into English, French and other languages, is a famous example of Renaissance neostoicism. Another is the treatise *On Constancy* published by the Flemish humanist Justus Lipsius in 1584 [45]. What attracted sixteenth-century readers in the Greek and Roman stoic philosophers, Seneca in particular, was their advice on preserving tranquillity of mind or 'constancy' in the face of tyranny, death or what

Hamlet calls 'the slings and arrows of outrageous fortune'. As an inscription on a sixteenth-century English portrait puts it,

> More than the rock amidst the raging seas
> The constant heart no danger dreads nor fears.

In similar fashion, Pamela, the heroine of Sidney's pastoral romance *Arcadia*, is described as standing firm 'like a rock amidst the sea, beaten both with the winds and with the waves, yet itself immovable'. The essentially passive virtue of constancy was more appropriate for the subjects of a monarch than for the politically active citizens of a republic. As in the case of stoicism, the revival of Roman law – the law of the Roman Empire, rather than the earlier Republic – became particularly important in the monarchies beyond the Alps. Roman law had been studied in the Middle Ages, at the university of Bologna in particular. In the fifteenth and six-teenth centuries, however, scholars became increasingly con-scious of the relation between this law and the society which had produced it, and of the changes in the legal system over time. A number of Italian humanists took an interest in ancient legal texts, but from the lawyer's point of view they were amateurs. The real advances were made by men who had been trained in law as well as in the humanities. Of the three leading figures in the reinterpretation of Roman law in the early sixteenth century, only one, Andrea Alciati, was an Italian, and he spent much of his life teaching in France, at the universities of Avignon and Bourges. Guillaume Budé was a Parisian, while Ulrich Zasius, who was a friend of Erasmus, came from the German city of Constance. If the first humanists to study Roman law were Italians, it was the French who made the greatest contribution in the long run [41]. This was appropriate enough, since French monarchs claimed, as Roman emperors had done, to be 'absolute', in other words above the laws, and it was a Roman jurist who declared that 'what pleases the prince has the force of law'.

A very different sphere in which northern or western Euro-peans are generally held to have surpassed their Italian mas-ters is that of prose fiction. In the case of comedy it was very difficult to do better than Ariosto and Aretino; in the epic,

44

to outdo Ariosto (which was the aim of Spenser in the *Faerie Queene*); in the pastoral, to improve on Tasso's *Aminta* or Gian Battista Guarini's *Pastor Fido* (1585), a romantic play about a faithful lover, which was much imitated all over Europe at the turn of the century. In the case of prose fiction (it is misleading to use the modern term 'novel'), the Italians from Boccaccio to Bandello, were masters of the short story, but the development of the genre into something more ambitious took place outside Italy. The great masters of the new form were of course Rabelais, with his *Pantagruel* (1532), *Gargantua* (1534) and his *Tiers Livre* (1546), and Cervantes, with his *Don Quixote* (in two parts, 1605 and 1615), but comparatively minor figures produced work of high quality, from Sir Philip Sidney's *Arcadia* (originally written *c*.1580) to the anonymous Spanish *Lazarillo de Tormes* (1554), which breaks with convention by telling the story of a professional beggar and trickster from the point of view of this unheroic hero [46: part 4].

These works of fiction owe a considerable debt to classical antiquity; to the comic dialogues of Lucian, to the Greek romances, such as *Daphnis and Chloe*, and above all to late Latin prose fiction, to the *Golden Ass* of Apuleius and the *Satyricon* of Petronius. They owe something to medieval romance, and in particular to the ironic rewriting of romance by Ariosto. However, what Rabelais and Cervantes actually produced is without parallel. One of the most novel features in the work of both men was the importance of parody; the parody of romances of chivalry in particular. A major theme in the romances was the quest for the grail; the heroes of Rabelais, on the other hand, undertake a kind of anti-quest for the 'Oracle of the Holy Bacbuc', which takes the form of a bottle. As for Don Quixote, who is decribed on the first page as a compulsive reader of romances of chivalry, his adventures are a comic transposition of the stories of knight errants with which his head is full. Both stories are concerned with the relation of fiction to reality, with the problem of interpretation. In the prologue to *Gargantua*, the author (a certain 'Master Alcofribas', according to the title page), suggests that the comic story contains a serious meaning, though he goes on to confuse the issue by making fun of people who find allegorical meanings in the poems of Homer. Cervantes too claims not to be inventing a story but retelling what he found in an Arab historian, and Don Quixote himself enacts the problems of interpretation by his persistence in treating ordinary life as if it were a romance of chivalry [48, 64, 73, 74].

It has been suggested that this ironic self-consciousness was encouraged by the rise of the printed book, and that it is 'print culture' which explains the main differences between Renaissance writers and those of the Middle Ages. Indeed, it is sometimes claimed that without printing there would have been no Renaissance at all [89]. The point is an important one, though easy to exaggerate or misinterpret. Since the invention of printing with movable type goes back only as far as the mid-fifteenth century, it is clear that it cannot have influenced the early Renaissance; the ideas of Petrarch and Alberti, the painting of Giotto and Masaccio, the architecture and the perspective of Brunelleschi. It is equally clear that the so-called 'diffusion' of the Renaissance was greatly facilitated by the new technology. In the case of the new forms of architecture, the importance of printed treatises (Vitruvius, Serlio, Palladio and so on) has already been stressed. Again, the fashion for the love-lyrics of Petrarch in aristocratic circles in the sixteenth century is almost inconceivable (on this scale, at least) without the presence of the elegant little volumes which young men and women can be seen holding in many painted portraits of the time [47]. Most obvious of all is the link between the revival of antiquity and availability in print of the classical writers.

A crucial role in this movement of revival was played by a group of scholar-printers in Italy, France, the Netherlands, Switzerland and elsewhere, who acted as middlemen between humanist scholars and the educated public. The great reputation enjoyed by Erasmus in his own day would have been inconceivable without the aid of print and printers such as Aldus Manutius of Venice or the Amerbachs and Frobens of Basel, whom he numbered among his friends. Some of these printers were scholars themselves. Aldus, for example, had studied the humanities at Ferrara and his elegant editions of Greek texts in the original language expressed a personal enthusiasm for the classics.

However, the place of print in the Renaissance was more than that of an agent of diffusion, important as this function was. It is hard to imagine how the textual criticism of the humanists (discussed above, p. 15) could have developed until there was a means of preserving as well as spreading emendations to texts. More generally, it has been argued that if the Carolingian Renaissance and the twelfth-century Renaissance burned themselves out within a relatively short time, while 'the' Renaissance lasted so much longer, the success of the latter must be attributed largely to print [89]. There is an obvious parallel with the history of heresy. The Reformation succeeded where medieval heresies failed because it had a mass-produced means of propagating new ideas.

Of course the Reformation did not spread by print alone, but by word of mouth as well, and the same can be said of the Renaissance. Small but influential discussion-groups like the Platonic Academy in Florence or the Palace Academy of Henri III of France are a reminder of the importance of orality in learned culture. The dialogue, one of the most important literary forms of the period (think of the *Colloquies* of Erasmus, More's *Utopia* and so on) was often modelled on actual discussions, and its style combines literary elements with what has been called 'oral residue' (it is hard to say whether orality is being assimilated by print, or print by orality). Again, some of the literary masterpieces of the Renaissance draw inspiration from traditional popular culture, which was an oral culture.

The *Praise of Folly* of Erasmus, for example, draws on a popular tradition of feasts of fools as well as on St Paul and the classical tradition of satire. In *Don Quixote*, Sancho Panza in particular belongs to a popular comic tradition. 'Panza' means 'paunch', and Sancho's rotundity is reminiscent of the figure of Carnival, while his tall thin master resembles Lent. Another carnivalesque figure from head to toe (or, since he cannot see his toes, head to belly) is Falstaff, and his abandonment by Prince Hal has been compared to the 'Trial of Carnival' with which the festive season often closed. Still more thoroughly carnivalesque is the *Gargantua and Pantagruel* of Rabelais; the giants, the trickster Panurge, the stress on feasting, drinking and defecating, the comedy of violence, and the use of the hyperbolic language of mountebanks [74]. The point is not that Rabelais was a popular writer; he was a learned man, a physician well-read in Greek and Latin literature, and his book is full of allusions which would have been incomprehensible to the craftsmen of Lyons (where his book was first published), or to the local peasants. What he does is to draw on popular culture for his own purposes, for example to mock the traditional learned culture of the hidebound theologians of the Sorbonne. The use of popular forms for subversive purposes was particularly common in the later Renaissance, the phase of disintegration, which the following section will discuss.

4 The Disintegration of the Renaissance

If it is difficult to say when the Renaissance began, it is quite impossible to say when it ended. Some scholars choose the 1520s, others 1600, 1620, 1630 or even later. It is always hard to say when a movement has come to an end, and this is doubly difficult when so many regions and arts are involved as in this case. 'End' is too sharp, too decisive a word. A better term, because it is a more precise one, might be 'disintegration'. The point is that what began as a movement of a few people with clear aims gradually lost its unity as it spread, so that in the course of time it becomes more and more difficult to decide who or what belongs to it.

In the visual arts, in Italy, the 1520s mark a transition from the High Renaissance to what art historians now call 'Mannerism', a tendency (rather than an organised movement) to place unusual emphasis on 'manner' or style; on novelty, difficulty, ingenuity, elegance and wit [57]. It was in the 1520s that work began on Michelangelo's Medici Chapel in Florence, the building described by the artist's pupil Vasari as 'extremely novel' because 'he departed a great deal from the kind of architecture regulated by proportion, order and rule that other artists made according to common usage and following Vitruvius and the works of antiquity'. Michelangelo rejected the classical orders, for example, for forms of his own. Towards the end of the same decade, Giulio Romano also broke the rules in his Palazzo de Te in Mantua; indeed, his deliberately 'ungrammatical' combinations of classical elements seem to have been intended to shock the spectator in a playful kind of way. They are in a sense 'anti-classical', although there were precedents in late classical antiquity for this kind of anti-classicism [22: chs 7, 9].

In the case of painting and sculpture it is harder to decide what should count as 'mannerist'. A rejection of the rules of proportion and perspective can be found in the paintings of Rosso, Pontormo and Parmigianino in the 1520s and 1530s, associated with a stylish but rather cold elegance which is also to be found in the portraits of Pontormo's pupil Bronzino. A similar rejection of the conventions, associated this time with expressive force, can be found in Michelangelo's *Last Judgement* (1536–41) in the Sistine Chapel. The artist is said to have remarked that all the rules of proportion and perspective are of no use 'without the eye', an idea which was elaborated into a theory by Giovan Paolo Lomazzo later in the century. In the case of sculpture, elongated figures in elegantly twisted poses ('snakelike', as Michelangelo called them, *figura serpentinata*), are the main criteria of the mannerist phase, which is generally taken to include Cellini's statue of Perseus and the salt-cellar he made for François I (both works of the 1540s), and Bartolommeo Ammannati's *Fountain of Neptune* in the Piazza della Signoria in Florence [19: chs 10–11]. The playful side of Mannerism is well exemplified in the art of gardens and grottoes (from which the term 'grotesque' is derived); the Boboli Gardens in Florence, for example, or the park at Bomarzo designed for the Roman aristocrat Vicino Orsini, which takes the form of a sixteenth-century Disneyland, with its stone monsters, its leaning tower, and its hell mouth (inside which can be found a marble picnic table).

The examples quoted so far, apart from Parmigianino, are Tuscan or Roman. In Venice, by contrast, Titian and his followers continued to work in the High Renaissance style in the 1520s and beyond. Tintoretto's absorption of a Michelangelesque style can be seen in his dramatic *St Mark Rescuing a Slave* of 1548, but Andrea Palladio followed the classical rules in the villas he was designing in the 1550s and 1560s, and Veronese went on working in the High Renaissance manner until his death in 1588.

In literature it is still more difficult, and less fruitful, to try to decide who was a mannerist and who was not. It is tempting to take Michelangelo's poems, Vasari's *Lives* and Cellini's autobiography as examples of literary mannerism because of what we know about the other activities of their authors. The pastoral dramas of Tasso and Guarini are also common choices. These pieces are certainly self-conscious and stylish; the problem is that the same adjectives apply to many earlier works of Renaissance literature. Guarini was criticised for trying to combine two genres, tragedy and pastoral, but the others do not flout the rules in the manner of Pontormo or Giulio Romano. They are not in this sense anti-classical. Music too poses a problem. The madrigals of the late sixteenth-century Sicilian prince, Carlo Gesualdo, are often described as 'mannerist', but the development of music was, as we have seen, out of phase with that of the other arts.

To identify mannerist works outside Italy is an even more difficult task. The main problem stems from the fact that although the 1520s were late in the career of the Renaissance in Italy, they were early in that movement's history in France, Spain, England, and Central and Eastern Europe. An ungrammatical building, like the palace built at Heidelberg in the 1550s, known after its patron as the Ottheinrichbau, may be the result of ignorance rather than sophistication. A case can be made for dating Mannerism relatively early in the Netherlands, but the best-known and least-disputed examples of the tendency outside Italy are as late as the 1580s, when El Greco began working for Philip II of Spain – who preferred Titian – while Bartholomaeus Spranger entered the service of the emperor Rudolf II [59]. To seek for literary mannerism outside Italy has little use except to reveal the ambiguities of the concept. Some critics would choose John Lyly's *Euphues* (1579) as a typical example, a romance written in a manner so elaborately idiosyncratic, and so widely imitated, that the term 'euphuism' had to be coined to describe it. Others would choose the poetry and prose of John Donne, whose style is a reaction against euphuism.

Again, the essays of Montaigne are sometimes discussed as 'Renaissance' productions, sometimes as part of a 'Counter-Renaissance' and sometimes as mannerist or even 'baroque'. It seems more useful to make the more modest point that Montaigne is a characteristically late Renaissance writer, who could not have done what he did had the earlier Renaissance not taken place, but does not share all the values of that phase of the movement. His relaxed style of writing, for example, is not artless (as it pretends to be), and it does not break with the classical tradition. It expresses a not uncommon reaction of the time against the dignified sentence structure of Cicero and in favour of the more informal style of Seneca. This deceptively simple style is also appropriate for a writer who maintains a detached, sceptical attitude in the face of the pretensions of kings and scholars and of grand claims for the dignity of man and the power of reason [70].

Whether we find the term 'Mannerism' useful, or prefer to use the more neutral 'Late Renaissance', the changes which took place require explanation. The explanations commonly given are of two opposite (though possibly complementary) kinds. In the first place, there are what may be called 'internalist' accounts, explanations in terms of the internal history or internal 'logic' of a particular genre. If we think of the history of Renaissance painting, as Vasari did, as the progressively more successful imitation of nature, then we may well wonder what could possibly follow the apogee of Leonardo, Raphael and early Michelangelo. If we think of the history of Renaissance architecture as the progressively more correct imitation of the rules of the ancients, a similar problem arises after the High Renaissance. Where could one go from there? In a late phase of any artistic or literary tradition a need to react against this tradition, which seems exhausted, is likely to be felt. In such a late phase, the public – spectators, readers, listeners – are likely to be more conscious of the conventions than their predecessors were, and thus to appreciate the allusiveness and wit of artists who are wilfully incorrect, who subvert or play with the rules.

In the second place, there are the 'externalist' explanations of changes in culture as a response to changes in society. In the case of Mannerism, the response is generally described in terms of 'crisis'; whether the crisis identified is religious, political or social. It was of course in the 1520s that Luther broke with the Church of Rome, while in 1527 the city of Rome was sacked by the army of Charles V [58]. These were traumatic events for many Italians, though not necessarily more traumatic than the 1490s, the decade of Savonarola's call for the reform of the Church and the French invasion of Italy. We know that Michelangelo took his religion very seriously and that he was tormented by doubts about his salvation. It is plausible enough to suggest relationships between his religious paintings and his religious ideas; rather less plausible to explain his architectural innovations in the same way [69]. Cellini's autobiography does not give the impression that its hero passed through a religious crisis, or that he found the Sack of Rome traumatic; he seems to have enjoyed it as an adventure. The stiff elegance of the men and women portrayed by Pontormo or Bronzino is sometimes treated as a symptom of the 'alienation' (of the artist or the sitter), but it may simply have been an attempt to render a currently fashionable Spanish style of aloof aristocratic behaviour. Generally speaking, so little is known about the inner lives of most artists in this period that it is unwise to make assumptions one way or the other.

Was Mannerism a response to a social crisis? Social crises are always difficult to define, let alone date, but there is at least evidence of a change in the social and political structure. In sixteenth-century Italy there does seem to have been a gradual shift of wealth and power away from merchants and towards the landowning class, a shift which Marxists describe as 'refeudalisation'. The independent city-states and their merchant patriciates which had made Italy such a distinctive part of Europe were replaced – Venice and Genoa apart – by courts and aristocracies. Elegant, sophisticated, playful and allusive, Mannerism is an aristocratic style.

Mannerism is sometimes characterised as an 'anti-Renaissance' or 'counter-Renaissance', but it might be better to describe it as a late phase of the Renaissance, since the breaking of the classic rules was not meant altogether seriously and in any case it assumed a knowledge of the very rules which were broken. If we turn to the humanists of the time, the scholars and the men of letters, we find that they were concerned not to break with the Renaissance past but rather to elaborate some aspects of it at the expense of others. Political writers, such as Giovanni Botero, whose *Reason of State* (1589) did a good deal to make that term fashionable, continued to comment on Roman history, but now turned to

Tacitus on the late Empire rather than Livy on the early Republic. 'Neoplatonism', as the cult of Plato is generally called, became fashionable in court circles in sixteenth-century Europe, from Paris to Prague, perhaps because a stress on the contemplative rather than on the active life suited the subjects of monarchies (as opposed to the citizens of republics). The neoplatonic movement involved not only an interest in the writings of Plato himself, but also in those of his late classical followers, such as Plotinus and Iamblichus, who had turned increasingly to mysticism and magic. There seems to have been an increasing concern with the 'occult philosophy' (as we would say, 'magic') and with 'natural philosophy' (in modern terms, 'science'), perhaps because these studies – which it is not yet possible to distinguish – offered an escape from the troubled world of man. The Polish canon Nicolaus Copernicus, the German Heinrich Cornelius Agrippa, the Englishman John Dee and the Italian Giordano Bruno (burned for heresy in Rome in 1600), were among the most famous of those who took this route [31, 55, 56].

Another response to crisis was the stoic revival discussed in section 3 above. The cult of constancy seems to have been at the height of its appeal in the second half of the sixteenth century, when the civil wars in France and the Netherlands made the tranquillity of mind recommended by Seneca and other stoic philosophers as necessary as it was difficult to attain. Others, like Montaigne, who became disillusioned with stoicism, turned to classical scepticism, to the doctrine that in an uncertain world the wise man does best to suspend judgement.

The later sixteenth century has also been called an 'age of criticism'. The term 'critic' was coming into use at the time, in the first place to describe the scholarly editors of classical texts, whose methods of discovering incorrect transcriptions were becoming increasingly sophisticated (the editions by Lipsius of his favourite authors, Tacitus and Seneca, are outstanding examples of this 'textual criticism'). The term was widening to include what we call 'literary criticism' and 'art criticism'. Vasari's *Lives* are among the most famous works of art criticism of the time in which the rival merits of painting and sculpture, colour and drawing, Titian and

Michelangelo, were hotly debated in Italy. Treatises were also written to attack or defend Dante, or to lay down the rules for writing epics or tragedies.

All these tendencies, from Platonism to criticism, have their parallels in fifteenth-century Italy, but the changes in emphasis give the late Renaissance a character of its own, whether or not we call it the 'age of Mannerism', or the 'autumn' of the Renaissance. Personally, I should prefer to describe the period not as one of 'decline' – the achievement of Michelangelo, Tasso, Montaigne, Shakespeare, Cervantes and others is too stupendous for that – but of 'disintegration' as defined at the beginning of this section, a disintegration spread over a long period.

Certain Renaissance elements – favourite attitudes, forms, themes and so on – long survived in European culture. In the reign of pope Urban VIII (1623–44), for example, there was a 'second Roman renaissance', modelled on the age of pope Leo X, the age of Bembo and Raphael. In France at this time, François de Sales and others have been described with good reason as 'pious humanists', while a certain Nicolas Faret made a success of publishing in 1630 a treatise on 'the art of pleasing at court' which was little more than a translation of sections from Castiglione's *Courtier*. As for England, there is much to be said for describing Robert Burton and Sir Thomas Browne as humanists in the Renaissance sense of the term. Burton's *Anatomy of Melancholy* (1621), opens with a reference to 'Man, the most excellent and noble creature of the world', and quotes endlessly from earlier Renaissance writers such as the philosopher Ficino as well as from Cicero and Seneca. Browne's *Religio Medici* (published 1642 but written in 1635), is a similar meditation on 'the dignity of humanity', as presented in classical texts.

If we include Burton and Browne, there is obviously a case for Sir William Temple, who defended the superiority of ancient learning and literature over the 'moderns' in an essay written in the 1690s. If we include Temple, there is obviously a case for including Swift (once Temple's secretary), and Dr Johnson, Pope, Burke and Gibbon, all of whom have been described as examples of Augustan 'humanism' [61]. After all, the 'Augustan' age of English culture, the eighteenth

55

century, derives its name from these writers' identification with ancient Roman culture in the time of Augustus. Dr Johnson's poem on London imitates a satire of the Roman writer Juvenal, while Gibbon's *Decline and Fall*, written in the age of the American Revolution, draws an implicit parallel between two declining empires, the Roman and the British. The themes of liberty and corruption so prominent in the political thought of the eighteenth century are at once an inheritance from Greece and Rome – via Renaissance Florence and Venice – and an adaptation of this heritage to the needs of an increasingly commercialised society [62].

Artists too continued to accept many of the values of the Italian Renaissance. Joshua Reynolds and George Romney both visited Italy to study classical sculpture and Renaissance painting (more especially the work of Raphael and Titian). Eighteenth-century English houses are called 'Palladian' because many of them were inspired by the villa designs of the sixteenth-century Italian architect Andrea Palladio.

There was a similar enthusiasm for antiquity in France, in the age of Louis XIV (not infrequently compared to Augustus), and again during the French Revolution, when the Roman Republic provided inspiration. In the early nineteenth century, as we have seen, the defenders of the classical tradition in education expressed their identification with Renaissance values by coining the term *Humanismus* [5].

These parallels with the fifteenth and sixteenth centuries are striking ones, and it would not be difficult to add to their number. However, the enthusiasm for antiquity and for Renaissance Italy was gradually changing its meaning as a result of other changes in culture and society. One of the greatest of these changes was the result of the movement historians often call the 'Scientific Revolution' of the seventeenth century, the work of Galileo, Descartes, Newton and many others. It was nothing less than a new picture of the universe in which the earth was no longer central, the heavens were no longer incorruptible, and the workings of the cosmos could be explained by the laws of mechanics. The investigation of nature was conducted on the basis of systematic observation and experiment rather than on the study of authoritative texts. Classical and renaissance views of the universe were rejected. The new discoveries were considered to demonstrate the superiority of 'moderns' over 'ancients' in some respects at least. The new world-view, as it spread, cut educated men off from the past. It is for such reasons as these that historians date the disintegration of the Renaissance to the 1620s and 1630s, the age of Galileo and Descartes. It should also be obvious why it has become impossible to share Jacob Burckhardt's view of the Renaissance as obviously 'modern' [1].

5 Conclusion

In this essay, the Renaissance has been defined rather more narrowly than it was by Burckhardt. It has been considered, to use Gombrich's useful distinction, as a 'movement' rather than as a 'period' [11]. Even as a movement, it has been circumscribed fairly tightly, with an emphasis (painting apart) on the attempt to revive antiquity, rather than on the other kinds of cultural change to which Burckhardt and many other historians have drawn attention. These limitations are deliberate. For one thing, a brief essay which deals with so many branches of learning and the arts and with so many European countries would become intolerably vague if it lacked a sharp focus. Still more important, however, is the fact that almost every other characteristic attributed to the Renaissance can also be found in the Middle Ages, to which it is so often contrasted. Obviously convenient for purposes of exposition, the simple binary opposition between Middle Ages and Renaissance is in many ways seriously misleading.

Take Burckhardt's famous 'development of the individual', for example (a concept about which he admitted to having doubts). The notion is not a very clear one. One of its meanings is self-assertiveness, the 'modern sense of fame' as Burckhardt called it. Competitiveness may have been particularly strong in Renaissance Florence – it is impossible to measure it – but as Huizinga pointed out, medieval knights cared a good deal about glory [76]. In their case too fame was the spur.

Another meaning of Renaissance 'individualism' is consciousness of individuality. It is always possible to draw attention, as Burckhardt did in his chapter on 'the discovery of the world and of men', to the rise of biographies and autobiographies in the Italian Renaissance, from the memoirs

59

of pope Pius II to the autobiography of Benvenuto Cellini, and also to the rise of portraits and self-portraits (such as Titian's and Dürer's). Yet autobiographies can also be found – if rather less frequently – in the Middle Ages. For this and other reasons it has been argued that the 'discovery of the individual' came in the twelfth century [77].

Another common way of characterising the Renaissance is in terms of reason; the human reason praised by the humanists, the rational ordering of space made possible by the discovery of perspective, or what Burckhardt called 'the spirit of calculation', illustrating it from the statistics collected by the Venetian Republic in the fifteenth century. Here too the division between Renaissance and Middle Ages has come to seem an artificial one. Rationalism, like individualism, is a slippery concept, but an interest in precise figures can be found in western Europe in the twelfth century, if not before [79]. It was encouraged by the growing employment of two kinds of calculating-machine, the abacus (which was in use in the eleventh century), and the mechanical clock (in use in the fourteenth). In other words, numeracy was not new in the age of Bruni and Brunelleschi. Indeed, it has become difficult to argue that there was any fundamental change in the psychology or mentality of even an educated minority between the Middle Ages and the Renaissance (whether this transition is placed around 1500, 1400 or 1300). At this point it may be worth pausing to take stock and to enquire whether the Renaissance may not be in danger of dissolving altogether, for two rather different kinds of reason.

In the first place, it was defined by Burckhardt as the beginning of modernity, a concept about which historians have become increasingly unhappy since his day, partly because it implies a simple evolutionary model of cultural change, which many of us now reject, and partly because in the last generation or so, westerners have come to think, more or less uneasily, that what they are living in is actually a 'post-modern' world. For anyone who holds such views, the Renaissance will seem rather more remote than it did [88].

In the second place, although the achievements of Petrarch, Leonardo and so many other artists, writers and scholars still compel admiration, it has become much harder than it was in Burckhardt's day to separate these achievements from those of the Middle Ages on one side and from those of the seventeenth and eighteenth centuries on the other. Aristotle, to take an obvious example, was the master of many European intellectuals from his rediscovery in the thirteenth century to his rejection some four hundred years later, and the humanist debates about his philosophy are easier to understand if they are considered in the context of this longer period [87]. Where does this leave us? There is no consensus. Some scholars in the field of what is still called 'Renaissance studies' go on as if nothing had happened. Others, including the present author, are trying to situate what was happening in four-teenth-century Florence, fifteenth-century Italy and six-teenth-century Europe in a sequence of connected changes between 1000 (or thereabouts) and 1800. These long-term developments might be described as the 'westernisation of the west' in the sense that they made upper-class Europeans, at least, increasingly different from other peoples, as the history of the 'discovery' and conquest of much of the globe was to reveal. Some of these developments were technological; the invention of firearms, mechanical clocks, printing, new kinds of sailing-ship and of machines which speeded up spinning and weaving. The changes which will be emphasised here, however, are changes in mentality, two in particular.

In an important study, the sociologist Norbert Elias has argued that the sixteenth century was a crucial period in the west for what he calls the 'civilising process', in other words the development of self-control, quoting among other evidence the treatises on good manners by Erasmus and by the Italian archbishop Giovanni Della Casa, both of them frequently reprinted in a number of languages [84]. There seems little doubt that concern for civilised behaviour at table (refraining from spitting, washing one's hands beforehand, and so on) was widely shared at that time, at least in certain social circles, but (as Elias admits) it is impossible to draw a sharp line between Renaissance and Middle Ages. Medieval books on 'courtesy' go back as far as the tenth century [80].

It should be emphasised that no one is suggesting that all other cultures (traditional Japan, for example, or China) lacked a sense of restraint at table and elsewhere. Western courtesy or civilisation was one set of conventions among others. It might therefore be more exact to talk of the rise of a sense of privacy, or of a gradual change in assumptions about the relative spheres of private and public, as the upper classes began to eat from individual plates rather than from communal dishes, to sit on individual chairs rather than communal benches, and to think it ill-mannered to offer a guest (to quote Della Casa's example), 'fruit from which you have already taken a bite'. These changes may well have something to do with Burckhardt's 'individualism', but they were spread thinly over a much longer period. They are perhaps associated with other forms of restraint or repression, notably the sexual repression which seems to have become a characteristic of western culture in this period.

A second approach to cultural changes in the medieval and early modern periods stresses the effect on mentalities of changes in the modes of communication. Historians of rhetoric have noted the increasing concern with the art of persuasion (whether by public speeches or private letters), revealed by the treatises on the subject produced in Italy in particular from the time of the Benedictine monk Alberic of Monte Cassino, at the end of the eleventh century [81]. Some of them would go so far as to speak of a 'rhetorical revolution' or even a 'language revolution' in the later Middle Ages, pointing out that philosophers were becoming conscious that the relation between language and reality was problematic. Rhetoric is a discipline concerned with gestures as well as words, and its study seems to have encouraged the sense of social role, the concern with the presentation of self so evident in Castiglione's *Courtier* or in the lives of men as different as Thomas More and Walter Raleigh [52, 63].

Others have stressed the spread of literacy in the Middle Ages for both commercial and administrative reasons. The self-consciousness which fascinated Burckhardt may have been one of the consequences of the new habits of solitary reading and writing [82]. Yet other historians place the emphasis on what they call 'print culture'. It is not always easy to distinguish between the consequences of printing and those of an earlier rise of literacy and numeracy, but at least it can be said that in the long run the invention of printing increased the availability of information, thus widening mental horizons and encouraging critical attitudes to authority by making the discrepancies between different authors more visible [89].

Why these particular changes should have taken place in this period is – like most fundamental questions in history – difficult to grasp, but it is at least possible to offer a few hypotheses. The concern with rhetoric developed in the city-states of northern Italy where the involvement of the citizens in government made the art of persuasion particularly necessary. The growth of international trade (in which Italy once again played a central role), encouraged literacy because of the need to record commercial transactions and to keep accounts. The development of centralised states also encouraged the use of written records and so increased the need for literacy. Norbert Elias has even suggested that the civilising process is ultimately connected with political centralisation. People are forced by the central power to live at peace with one another and more gradually to exercise restraint in other ways as well. The increasing concern with military discipline (including drill) in the sixteenth century is one argument in favour of this hypothesis, and the neostoic movement, discussed earlier, demonstrates the link between the cult of self-control and the growing interest in particular ancient writers, Seneca in particular [45]. For the later classical world had also been centralised, and many of the 'new' problems which arose between the eleventh and eighteenth centuries had also been 'ancient' ones. A debate over civilisation, or courtesy, for example, had already taken place (in terms of *urbanitas* or 'urbanity') in the Rome of Cicero.

As these examples suggest, the appeal of the classics in the whole period, and in the fifteenth and sixteenth centuries in particular, was largely the result of their practical relevance. The ancients were admired because they were guides to living. Following them meant travelling with more security in the direction in which people were already going.

Select Bibliography

For recent work in Renaissance studies, it is worth consulting the specialist journals, such as the *Journal of the Warburg and Courtauld Institutes*, the *Journal of Medieval and Renaissance Studies*, the *Bulletin of the Society for Renaissance Studies*, and *Bibliothèque d'humanisme et renaissance* (which includes articles in English)

Introductions

[1] J. Burckhardt, *The Civilisation of the Renaissance in Italy* (English trans. 1944; first published in German in 1860), remains indispensable, although many of the conclusions have been challenged.

[2] D. Hay, *The Italian Renaissance in its Historical Background* (second edn, Cambridge, 1977). A balanced survey.

[3] E.H. Gombrich, *The Story of Art* (14th edn, 1984), chs 12–18.

[4] E. Panofsky, *Renaissance and Renascences in Western Art* (1970). This lucid and elegant essay places the Renaissance in the long history of classical revivals.

[5] P.O. Kristeller, *Renaissance Thought* (New York, 1961). A classic account.

[6] P. Burke, *Culture and Society in Renaissance Italy* (1972; revised edn, 1987). Attempts to replace the arts in their social context.

[7] L. Martines, *Power and Imagination: City-States in Renaissance Italy* (1980). Crude but vigorous and especially useful on continuities between the twelfth and thirteenth centuries and the Renaissance.

[8] J. Hale (ed.), *A Concise Encyclopaedia of the Italian Renaissance* (1981). A useful work of reference.

The Idea of the Renaissance

[9] J. Huizinga, 'The problem of the Renaissance' (1920), repr. in his *Men and Ideas* (New York, 1959). The reflections of a great Dutch historian.

[10] W.K. Ferguson, *The Renaissance in Historical Thought* (Cambridge, Mass., 1948). From the humanists onward.

[11] E.H. Gombrich, 'The Renaissance – Period or Movement?' in *Background to the English Renaissance*, ed. J.B. Trapp (1974).

Italy: Painting

[12] E. Panofsky, *Studies in Iconology* (New York, 1939). The most celebrated example of the 'iconographical' approach to meaning in the visual arts.

[13] E. Wind, *Pagan Mysteries in the Renaissance* (revised edn, Oxford, 1980). Learned and ingenious neoplatonic interpretations of Botticelli, Titian, etc.

[14] E.H. Gombrich, *Symbolic Images* (1972). A more sceptical approach to the same cluster of problems.

[15] M. Baxandall, *Painting and Experience in Fifteenth Century Italy* (Oxford, 1972). A historical anthropology of visual communication.

[16] C. Hope, 'Artists, patrons and advisers in the Italian Renaissance', in *Patronage in the Renaissance*, ed. G.F. Lytle and S. Orgel (Princeton, 1981). A critique of the recent emphasis on learned programmes for paintings.

[17] B. Cole, *The Renaissance Artist at Work* (1983). Deals with training, raw materials and genres.

[18] S. Edgerton, *The Renaissance Rediscovery of Linear Perspective* (New York, 1975).

Italy: Sculpture and Architecture

[19] C. Avery, *Florentine Renaissance Sculpture* (1970). A brief introduction.

[20] C. Seymour, *Sculpture in Italy 1400–1500* (Harmondsworth, 1966). A full survey.
[21] R. Wittkower, *Architectural Principles in the Age of Humanism* (1949). Does for architecture what Panofsky did for painting.
[22] P. Murray, *The Architecture of the Italian Renaissance* (1963). A lucid and businesslike introduction.
[23] L. Heydenreich and W. Lotz, *Architecture in Italy 1400–1600* (Harmondsworth, 1974). A thorough scrutiny.

Italy: Intellectual History

[24] E. Garin, *Italian Humanism* (1965). First published in 1947, frequently criticised, but not yet superseded.
[25] H. Baron, *The Crisis of the Early Italian Renaissance* (Princeton, 1955). Stresses the links between republican politics and 'civic humanism'.
[26] J. Seigel, 'Civic humanism or Ciceronian rhetoric?' *Past and Present*, 34 (1966). A critique of Baron.
[27] W.G. Craven, *Giovanni Pico della Mirandola* (Geneva, 1981).
[28] A. Grafton and L. Jardine, 'Humanism and the School of Guarino', *Past and Present*, 96 (1982). A critique of Garin and a discussion of education in theory and practice.
[29] F. Gilbert, *Machiavelli and Guicciardini* (Princeton, 1965). A penetrating study of two major figures on the edge of humanism.
[30] C.L. Stinger, *Humanism and the Church Fathers* (Albany, 1977).
[31] F. Yates, *Giordano Bruno and the Hermetic Tradition* (1964). Stresses humanist interest in the occult.
[32] E. Garin, *Astrology in the Renaissance* (1983).
[3] P.L. Rose, *The Italian Renaissance of Mathematics* (Geneva, 1975).

Renaissance Outside Italy: Visual Arts

[34] E. Rosenthal, 'The diffusion of the Italian Renaissance style in western Europe', *Sixteenth-Century Journal*, 9 (1978).

[35] A. Blunt, *Art and Architecture in France* (fourth edn, Harmondsworth, 1980).

[36] M. Baxandall, *The Limewood Sculptors of Renaissance Germany* (1980). Of much wider interest than the title might suggest.

[37] J. Bialostocki, *Art of the Renaissance in Eastern Europe* (1976). A fine study of the 'reception' of Italian forms.

[38] R.J. Knecht, 'Francis I: Prince and Patron' in *The Courts of Europe*, ed. A.G. Dickens (1980).

Renaissance Outside Italy: Ideas

[39] D.P. Walker, *The Ancient Theology* (1972). On attempts to reconcile neoplatonism with Christianity.

[40] F. Yates, *Astraea* (1975). Important essays on the political meanings of festivals, poetry, painting, etc. in England and France.

[41] D. Kelley, *Foundations of Modern Historical Scholarship* (New York, 1970). Deals with the relationship between language, law and history in the thought of French humanists.

[42] Q. Skinner, *Foundations of Modern Political Thought* (2 vols, Cambridge, 1978).

[43] J. Bentley, *Humanists and Holy Writ* (Princeton, 1983), surveys sixteenth-century New Testament scholarship.

[44] G. Kipling, *The Triumph of Honour: Burgundian Origins of the Elizabethan Renaissance* (Leiden, 1977).

[45] G. Oestreich, *Neostoicism and the Early Modern State* (Cambridge, 1982). Especially concerned with the Netherlands and with Justus Lipsius.

Literature

[46] A.J. Krailsheimer (ed.), *The Continental Renaissance* (Harmondsworth, 1971). Introductory survey of France, Germany, Italy and Spain.

[47] L. Forster, *The Icy Fire* (Cambridge, 1969). A comparative study of Petrarchism.

[48] T. Cave, *The Cornucopian Text* (Oxford, 1979). Discusses awareness of the problems of writing in Erasmus, Rabelais, Ronsard and Montaigne.

[49] T. Greene, *The Light in Troy* (1982). On imitation and assimilation in Italian, French and English poetry.

[50] D. Javitch, *Poetry and Courtliness in Renaissance England* (Princeton, 1978). On Sidney, Spenser, etc.

[51] S. Orgel, *The Illusion of Power* (Berkeley and Los Angeles, 1975). On theatre and politics in the English Renaissance.

[52] S. Greenblatt, *Renaissance Self-Fashioning from More to Shakespeare* (1980). A new look at Renaissance individualism.

Music and Science

[53] C. Palisca, *Humanism in Italian Renaissance Musical Thought* (New Haven, 1985).

[54] E. Lowinsky, 'Music in the culture of the Renaissance', *Journal of the History of Ideas*, 15 (1954).

[55] A. Debus, *Man and Nature in the Renaissance* (Cambridge, 1978). General survey, particularly useful on alchemy.

[56] M.B. Hall, 'Problems of the scientific Renaissance', in D. Hay *et al.*, *The Renaissance* (1982).

The Disintegration of the Renaissance

[57] J. Shearman, *Mannerism* (Harmondsworth, 1967). A lively survey of all the arts.

[58] A. Chastel, *The Sack of Rome* (Princeton, 1983). On the cultural consequences of the catastrophe of 1527.

[59] R.J.W. Evans, *Rudolf II and his World* (Oxford, 1973). Discusses humanism and Mannerism.

[60] R.R. Bolgar (ed.), *Classical influences on European Culture 1500–1700* (Cambridge, 1976). Follows the fortunes of the classical tradition.

[61] P. Fussell, *The Rhetorical World of Augustan Humanism* (Oxford, 1965). Presents Swift, Pope, Johnson, Reynolds, Gibbon and Burke as late Renaissance humanists.

[62] J. Pocock, *The Machiavellian Moment* (Princeton, 1975). Includes an important discussion of civic humanism in Anglo-American thought in the seventeenth and eighteenth centuries.

Individuals

[63] R.W. Hanning and D. Rosand (eds), *Castiglione: the Ideal and the Real in Renaissance Culture* (1983).

[64] P. Russell, *Cervantes* (1985).

[65] E. Panofsky, *Albrecht Dürer* (fourth edn, Princeton, 1955).

[66] J. McConica, *Erasmus* (1986).

[67] M. Kemp, *Leonardo da Vinci* (1981).

[68] Q. Skinner, *Machiavelli* (1980).

[69] H. Hibbard, *Michelangelo* (1975).

[70] P. Burke, *Montaigne* (1981).

[71] A. Fox, *Thomas More: History and Providence* (1982).

[72] N. Mann, *Petrarch* (1985).

[73] M.M. Screech, *Rabelais* (1979).

[74] M. Bakhtin, *Rabelais and his World* (1965: English trans., Cambridge, Mass., 1968).

[75] R. Jones and N. Penny, *Raphael* (1983).

Middle Ages

[76] J. Huizinga, *The Waning of the Middle Ages* (1919: English trans., 1924).

[77] C. Morris, *The Discovery of the Individual: 1050–1200* (1972).

[78] C. Brooke, *The Twelfth-Century Renaissance* (1969).

[79] A. Murray, *Reason and Society in the Middle Ages* (Oxford, 1978).

[80] C.S. Jaeger, *The Origins of Courtliness* (Philadelphia, 1985).

[81] J.J. Murphy, *Rhetoric in the Middle Ages* (Berkeley, 1974).

[82] H.J. Chaytor, *From Script to Print* (Cambridge, 1945).

[83] R. Bolgar (ed.), *Classical Influences on European Culture 500–1500* (Cambridge, 1971).

Conclusion

[84] N. Elias, *The History of Manners* (1939: English trans., Oxford, 1978).

[85] A. Toynbee, *A Study of History*, 9 (Oxford, 1954).

[86] L.D. Reynolds and N.G. Wilson, *Scribes and Scholars* (second edn, Oxford, 1974).

[87] C. Schmitt, 'Towards a reassessment of Renaissance Aristotelianism', *History of Science*, 11 (1973).

[88] W. Bouwsma, 'The Renaissance and the drama of European history', *American Historical Review*, 84 (1979).

[89] E. Eisenstein, *The Printing Revolution* (Cambridge, 1983).

Index

74